own story of finding herself in tears, despite a seemingly perfect life, and feeling a relatable longing. Through her efforts to explore what matters in life and her learnings, the book makes us pause and work through the things we have known inside all along."

—Kathi Nidd, *Readers' Favorite*, 5-Star Review

"Honest, authentic, and bomb-ass. Beyond bubbles and daily affirmations, Kalia debunks classic, superficial, self-care, commercial myths. She whips out 'truth-bombs' to stop your inner critic and promote your inner badass. She inspires you to be brave, bold, and bound by the relentless pursuit of YOUR personal joy, happiness, and real-live-no-jive-success across all facets of life. Learn through bite-sized kernels of wisdom and simple practices presented as a truth-telling pep talk straight from your bestie."

—K. Melissa Kennedy, Founder, Festival Food Tours,
https://www.festivalfoodtours.com/

"The world comes at you fast, and this book is a rubric for how to take ownership to hop in the driver's seat. The truth bombs sprinkled throughout keep you accountable to the work they lay out for you. One of the best lessons for where I am in life is that if you can do something, do it. If you can't, let it go. Both are options that do not require spending too much time worrying. My earth suit no longer supports worrying!"

—Karen Collins, Founder & CEO, Empowerlead,
Author of *Day One*, www.empower-lead.com

Advance Praise for *The Well Within*

"With warmth and wit, Kalia shares relatable stories and practical strategies, backed by research, to guide readers on a mindful journey of self-compassionate growth. The gently probing questions in each bite-sized chapter lead the reader by the hand, like a wise friend, inward and outward. She goes beyond introspection, investigating not only our internal milieu, but also how environmental factors influence our inner world. I appreciate Kalia's recognition that being 'well within' isn't solely for our own sake, but so that we can bless others out of our abundance."

—Dr. Flora Brewington, Board Certified Family Physician

"Filled with truth bombs, life lessons, relatable anecdotes, and tangible takeaways, *The Well Within* serves as a powerful reminder for how to come back to yourself. Whether you're seeking guidance or already thriving, Kalia Garrido offers sage advice for everyday living to elicit even more personal power. This is the perfect new self-help book to motivate and inspire you."

—Brie Doyle, Author of *You Should Leave Now: Going on Retreat to Find Your Way Back to Yourself,* Founder of She Glows Retreats, www.BrieDoyle.com

"*The Well Within* by Kalia Garrido is a pitch-perfect resource for anyone interested in unlocking their personal power and turning their dreams into reality through radical self-care. The guidance offered is rooted in the feminine perspective, but Garrido makes it clear from the start that her suggestions are meant to be inclusive of all readers. The result is an insightful, potentially life-altering guide to improvising one's quality of life ... This is a book that readers will want to return to over and over again! Garrido's truths are incontrovertible and timeless, and the help she offers is real."

—Rich Follett, *Readers' Favorite*, 5-Star Review

"As an entrepreneur, recovering people pleaser, and woman who has spent a lifetime sprinting ahead, Garrido's message in *The Well Within* rings loud and clear. This book is a game changer for anyone (I'm looking at the entrepreneurs, leaders, and executives out there) who needs to hit the reset button and derail your current trajectory toward burnout. This is about making a true commitment to taking care of yourself so you can confidently wake up each day and handle the hundreds of challenges that are tossed at you every day."

—Kate Bailey, Founder, TARRA, TARRA.co

"Reading *The Well Within* is like snuggling up on the couch for a deep conversation with your authentically grounded and wise, truth-telling best friend. Kalia keeps it real while gently reminding us what we all know at the soul level ... that we are worthy of slowing down and looking inward, nourishing our bodies and minds—and loving ourselves well."

—Julie Hudson, Founder, mindfulhaus.com

"*The Well Within* takes well-known and less-known concepts for finding our true selves and compiles them into a concise read, guiding us to turn our attention inward to help ourselves, those we love, and the world around us. Kalia Garrido pulls us into focus with loving, open-minded, and knowledgeable tips sent from a place of deep understanding. Writing from the heart, Garrido offers her

THE
Well
WITHIN

UNLOCKING YOUR PERSONAL POWER
THROUGH RADICAL SELF-CARE

THE
Well
WITHIN

UNLOCKING YOUR PERSONAL POWER
THROUGH RADICAL SELF-CARE

KALIA GARRIDO

MERRY DISSONANCE PRESS   CASTLE ROCK, COLORADO

The Well Within: Unlocking Your Personal Power Through Radical Self-Care
Published by Merry Dissonance Press, LLC
Castle Rock, CO

www.HealthyWomenLeaders.com

FIRST EDITION
2024

Publisher's Cataloging-in-Publication
(Provided by Cassidy Cataloguing Services, Inc.)

Names: Garrido, Kalia, author.
Title: The well within : unlocking your personal power
through radical self-care / Kalia Garrido.
Description: First edition. | Castle Rock, Colorado : Merry
Dissonance Press, [2024]
Identifiers: ISBN: 978-1-939919-69-4
Subjects: LCSH: Self-actualization (Psychology) | Self-realization. | Self-care,
Health. | Mind and body. | Mental health. | Self-realization. | Self-esteem. |
Successful people--Psychological aspects. | Change (Psychology) | Control
(Psychology) | LCGFT: Self-help publications. | BISAC: BODY, MIND & SPIRIT
/ Inspiration & Personal Growth. | SELF-HELP / Personal Growth / General.
Classification: LCC: BF637.S4 G37 2024 | DDC: 158.1--dc23

ISBN 978-1-939919-69-4

Book Interior and Cover Design © 2024
Cover Design by Victoria Wolf, wolfdesignandmarketing.com
Book Design by Victoria Wolf, wolfdesignandmarketing.com
Editing by Donna Mazzitelli, writingwithdonna.com

I dedicate this book to all the deeply inspirational, rule-breaking, hardworking, big-dreaming women who have walked before me, to those who will walk after me, but most of all, to those who walk with me. You are worth the work.

Above all else, I dedicate this book to my daughter, Zenaya. This is some of what I've learned along the way. Take these teachings, build on them, and develop your own. Never stop seeking out the extraordinary. I wish you a life beyond your wildest dreams.

CONTENTS

INTRODUCTION

My Wake-Up Call 1

Finding Depth 5

Definitions and Considerations 11

How to Use This Book 17

THE FIVE KEY LIFE LESSONS

LIFE LESSON 1: TRULY KNOW YOURSELF

Chapter 1: The Power of the Pause 29

Chapter 2: Learn to Listen to Yourself 35

Chapter 3: What's Within Your Control? 43

LIFE LESSON 2: WATCH WHAT YOU TAKE ON AND IN

Chapter 4: What Are You Consuming Physically? 57

Chapter 5: What Are You Consuming Mentally? 63

Chapter 6: How Do You Feel in Your Home Environment? .. 77

LIFE LESSON 3: WATCH WHAT YOU GIVE OUT

Chapter 7: Emotional Weather Patterns 93

Chapter 8: Stop Rushing 107

Chapter 9: Start Helping 115

LIFE LESSON 4: TREAT YOURSELF LOVINGLY

Chapter 10: Treat Yourself Physically 131

Chapter 11: Treat Yourself Mentally 139

Chapter 12: Apply Your Medicine 149

LIFE LESSON 5: EXPECT THE AWESOME

Chapter 13: Living Life on PURPOSE 163

Chapter 14: Believing in Yourself 177

Chapter 15: Believing in the Benevolent 189

CONCLUSION

A New Way of Living 199

Notes 207

Acknowledgments 211

About the Author 213

Invite Kalia to your Book Club! 215

Stay Connected! 217

About the Press 219

INTRODUCTION

*"I am not afraid of storms, for I am
learning how to sail my ship."* [1]

—Louisa May Alcott, American novelist and
poet, abolitionist, feminist, and suffragette

MY WAKE-UP CALL

A FEW YEARS BACK, on a beautiful late spring day, I left the gym after a great workout and proceeded to have an unprompted, magnificently ugly crying episode in my car. A waterfall of tears, a river of snot, and a windstorm of gasping, shuddering breaths ensued. In addition to this impressive physical display, there was also my utter mental confusion because I didn't know *why* I was so upset. Not a good look in the busy gym parking lot in a car with un-tinted windows.

I tried to unpack what was happening. I didn't feel depressed. In fact, I felt like I was finally living life on my own terms. I had recently left my corporate job to start my first business with my super smart and loving husband. We had healthy children. We lived in a beautiful home. Honestly, my life looked pretty sweet.

Moreover, I had always benchmarked how "healthy" I was by how many times I had been to the gym that week or how I felt in my jeans. Lately, I had been crushing my workouts, so what was going on?

That day in my car was not my first breakdown during that period of my life. I had experienced a variety of breakdowns in lots of places over the past few months. I had cried while folding laundry in my bedroom, on the kitchen floor after a not-so-graceful plop to my butt, and I was well versed in the classic shower cry.

From the outside in, I was living a dream. From the inside out, though, there was a building swell of stress. In truth, I was straining to hold it all together.

I wondered how I'd gotten here. I had followed society's prescription up to that point; I was right on track in the standard-issue "Roadmap to the Perfect Life." Why then was I feeling adrift and unfulfilled, like something big was missing? Turns out, that roadmap wasn't enough for me to live a whole, healthy, and fulfilling life. There was another roadmap, something far more subjective, more personal and deeper, that I had to discover for myself. The crying fits, the feelings of stress and confusion: those were the first signs of a major wake-up call to begin doing my *real* work, my inner work, to understand who I really was.

I also had to look at why the life I thought I wanted wasn't working. When I left my corporate career to start my first business, a software development shop, *man,* did I have on rose-colored glasses! I was so eager and excited to take on the world. But as any entrepreneur would tell you, it wasn't long before the stress of running the business took a serious toll. Add to that family responsibilities, including a new baby, and I was officially in over my head. The pressure of running the day-to-day business was intense. It involved selling to new clients, keeping existing clients happy, hiring, firing, and salary setting for employees. Our daughter was a wonderful baby, but like most new parents, sleep was in short supply, and the demands of working full time from home with a child were significant. I was smacked down with an unprecedented level of stress and anxiety that left me feeling adrift. My rose-colored glasses lay shattered in the gutter.

When we as human beings get into these darker places, we have two choices. The first is that we can allow that darkness to continue to advance, creeping on and in until we are in jeopardy of losing ourselves. The second is that we can take a stand against those negative feelings. The good news here is that we can choose to fight against this darkness anytime we want. Even if we are not ready to do that today, or tomorrow, or the next hundred times, there will always be another opportunity to decide it's time for things to change.

In my case, I wasn't going to give up my business or my family so something else had to shift. But what? The gym—and physical exercise—had always been the go-to for me when things got rough. But this new level of stress meant that going to the gym was no longer enough to "fix" me. I knew I needed to feel better, but I had no idea where to begin.

So I searched. I asked dozens of other women how they stayed healthy in their most stress-filled times. I researched articles, books, podcasts, and videos. I looked deeper and deeper within myself and became more or less obsessed with my inner workings. Over time, things became clearer.

What I uncovered was that I had to broaden my definition of what "being healthy" actually meant. In addition to feeling physically fit, there were other facets of health that I had been grossly ignoring, like mental, emotional, and spiritual health. Self-care had never been a focus for me. I needed to address these imbalances and commit to caring for my own well-being as an ongoing, nonnegotiable priority in my busy life.

As simple as this sounds now, at that time I felt I had unlocked something huge. By choosing to prioritize and care for myself with the same level of effort and attention that I gave to my other responsibilities, I began to feel much better. And the better I felt, the better I was able to show up for everything else that demanded my attention.

FINDING DEPTH

HERE'S SOMETHING THAT WILL NOT SHOCK anyone who has been paying attention: day-to-day life in our current society can be really tough. Outside influences are negative, obtrusive, and unending. There is a massive political divide, plenty of disease, hatred, and fighting. People can be just flat-out *horrible* to each other, and the worst of the worst is highlighted on the internet and news outlets every day.

Internal pressures, responsibilities, and obligations run high, and it feels like there is never enough time or energy to juggle it all. We scuttle around from task to task and give much of ourselves away without taking the time to refuel. As a result, we wind up getting stretched thin to the point of snapping. This is what happened to me. I found myself in a mental place I didn't like.

The *Oxford English Dictionary* defines the word "surface" as the outermost part of a solid object. That's a great way to describe where I operated from prior to my emotional breakdown. I stayed on or near the surface of life, just like so many of us do. I didn't dig deeper into what was happening around me or to me. I was okay on the sidelines. I went with the flow and kept up with the day-to-day. I wasn't searching for meaning or true understanding. Not only did I not know *how* to do that, but I also didn't even know anyone *could* do that.

LEAVING THE SURFACE

When I heard the call to do my inner work, it became important for me to get off the sidelines and start to explore. This is when life got complicated, though, because leaving the status quo introduced the risk of the unknown.

Humans are hardwired to avoid being hurt. Since we were children, we were told what to do to stay safe—until we believed it, embodied it, and likely preached it to our own kids. Better to stay where we are, unhurt, than risk what could happen with a new experience or a new way of living.

In *The Well Within*, my goal is to help you remove yourself from your "safe" zone and lead you gently into the deep end of life. I want to show you what I've uncovered: that this life is a precious gift, a beautiful piece of raw clay you can shape and mold to create whatever you want.

When I began my search, I felt scattered, messy, and alone. I now understand that this is a common experience for many people. When we experience an awakening of any sort, the life we are living, no matter how nice it looks or how comfortable it feels, is likely overdue for change.

Truth Bomb:

Safety is a myth.

Despite what you may hear or feel, nothing is ever actually "safe." Condoms can break. You could get hit by a car walking across your usually quiet street. Your heart can get broken by the one you trusted the most. Ironically enough, playing it safe puts you at an even greater risk—the risk of missing out on life. Playing it safe often means forgoing life experiences and opportunities that would help you grow.

Since you chose to pick up this book, maybe you are going through some version of unrest as well. Though it may not feel like it, this inner discontent is actually a great gift, as it will lead you into the true depths of yourself, where your personal power and pure potential are always accessible.

Some questions to consider at the beginning of this journey include:

* ✳ Do you ever feel swept away in the tide of daily life?
* ✳ Do you find yourself rushing around in Go! Go! Go! mode all the time?
* ✳ Are you yearning for something deeper than your day-in-day-out schedule?
* ✳ Do you prioritize everyone else before yourself?
* ✳ Do you feel a lack of fulfillment?
* ✳ Are you done with *just* getting by and ready to graduate to flourishing?
* ✳ Are you ready for a shake-up?

If you feel a yes to any of these questions, it may be an indication that you are ready to uncover the deeper significance in your life. Answering yes may be a clear signal that you are ready to enter the depths within to understand the feelings you've been experiencing.

These sneaky feelings of discontent ebb and flow; they flare up and they fade away. They take advantage of your low moments to get louder. They love stalking you in the middle of the night. But no matter how loud they get, they can be silenced by allowing yourself to be numbed by the routine of daily life.

Here are some of my favorite methods of avoiding or silencing my big inner feelings:

* Throwing myself into work
* Going into parenting overdrive
* Having an extra drink (or two)
* Going for run after run after run
* Wasting lots of time doom-scrolling on my phone
* Increasing my news intake
* Focusing my attention on (aka *judging*) other people
* Benchmarking myself against people I know

As you may have guessed, these methods only cover up the issues. They let us remain in denial and largely "asleep" through the few precious years we get to experience on this beautiful planet.

A life lived from the "La-la-la, I can't hear you" place, pushing your hands against your ears and refusing to address whatever issues may be shadowing you is precarious; it's a fragile way to live. Not only are you unaware of the issues, but you are vulnerable to outside influences and other people's agendas, relying on them to tell you how worthy (or not) you really are. Worst of all, you'll never know what you are truly capable of.

I know now that by shifting our focus inward and taking better care of ourselves, we will feel better about life. We can create the life we've dreamed of. We can switch our "I wish I had ____" thoughts into "Thank you for ____" moments.

DEFINITIONS AND CONSIDERATIONS

THE WELL WITHIN DEFINED

If you desire real change in your life, you must dive deep into what I call the *well within*. The well within is your personal and unique multidimensional inner world. It contains your innermost complexities, including your thoughts, emotions, beliefs, values, and memories, which have been developed from your life experiences. These are the informational building blocks that shape your perception of yourself and your sentiment of the world around you.

Going deeper underneath that initial layer of the personal-to-you internal particulars, the well within opens to an unlimited cavern with the blank-slate, never-ending potential for deep love and true joy that is not at all dependent on the people or conditions outside yourself. It is where your intuition comes from—the innate ability to understand or know something instinctively without the need for conscious reasoning. Your big ideas come from here. Your true healing comes from here. This is where your personal power lives, the kind that can never be extinguished. It is where your strength and courage come from. It is the space where your unique magic lives.

Successfully understanding and working through the information in the personal top layer allows you to throw open the cellar doors to the bottom layer and uncap the pure potential and power within.

Although everyone has the well within, most people live their lives without fully knowing, exploring, or living from this place of pure potential. I assure you of this: going within is an unavoidable part of the journey to truly thrive. The moment you commit to the action needed to effect real change in your life is the same moment you start unlocking your personal power.

A NEW DEFINITION OF RADICAL SELF-CARE

The term "self-care," in my humble opinion, is largely misused and under-defined. According to the *Oxford English Dictionary* definition, self-care is "the activity of taking care of one's own health, appearance, or well-being." Okay, I can get down with that. However, looking at how it's largely used, it becomes more of a casual, superficial Band-Aid that describes singular, one-off actions that are time-boxed and sit outside of daily life. A woman peacefully soaking in a bubble bath is the quintessential picture of self-care. Getting a massage or a facial is self-care. Those actions are good, yes, but real, radical self-care is different.

Radical self-care is a holistic, multifaceted, and intentional practice that requires self-prioritization at a transformative level. It involves taking a stand to actively consider and care for yourself from a physical, mental, emotional, and spiritual perspective. Radical self-care also includes diving into the root causes of stress, discomfort, and imbalance in your life. It will deeply challenge you to become healthier, happier, and more peaceful in a sustainable way.

Radical self-care emphasizes self-compassion, self-awareness, and self-empowerment. It involves setting healthy boundaries, saying no when needed, and taking care of yourself as a nonnegotiable part of your routine. It also involves engaging in activities that nourish and support your overall well-being, such as exercise, healthy eating, restorative sleep, mindfulness, and meaningful connections with others.

Radical self-care is about honoring and valuing yourself unapologetically and recognizing that taking care of yourself is not selfish; it's a vital act of self-preservation and self-love. It is a lifelong practice that requires deep self-reflection, critical self-awareness, and extreme self-compassion. It can lead to profound personal growth, resiliency, and a striking improvement in overall well-being.

In *The Well Within*, we will look at how radical self-care can be woven into the fabric of daily life. You will begin to experience a new perspective on how deep radical self-care runs and how it must be practiced with regularity and intention. If this sounds like a big deal, that's good—because it is. As with any paradigm shift, it can be difficult to adopt, but when you stick with it, you will be rewarded with a life lived beyond what you previously thought was possible.

WHAT I AM AND WHAT I'M NOT

In case there are any questions about my qualifications, let me address them here:

Just like so many of you, I am a hardworking, professional businesswoman who has climbed the career ladder with determination and commitment. I am a mother of two. I am a wife to a swamped tech executive husband. I am also a daughter to two loving parents, sister to my three siblings, and friend to a wide swath of amazing human beings.

As a woman who found herself over- and underwhelmed by the "perfect life," I decided to go on a quest for more. I took the time and did the work to face my personal darkness so I could find my footing. As a student of life and a human being driving my one precious Earth Suit, I am on a lifelong quest to thrive.

What I am not is a doctor, psychologist, nutritionist, meditation teacher, or a spiritual guide. So please take what I offer with the following disclaimer: This is what worked for me, and though I have a sense that it will work for you, too, I recognize that our cultures, upbringings, life experiences, and values may not align. We are all on our individual unique journeys, and I would never assume that your story is the same as mine. However, I would also never discount that we are all humans living at the same moment in history, trying to make our way along rocky, crisscrossed paths across the same planet Earth.

HEALTHY WOMEN LEADERS

Additionally, I am a lifelong "collector" of amazing women. I have always sought information, mentorship, and guidance from powerful, confident, passionate women who have come before me. Deep inside, I have what feels like an infinite hunger that needs to be filled with stories from other women who have figured something out about how to flourish. I look first to women because that is my personal experience, and it is where I find my greatest source of inspiration.

When I began my personal quest to climb out from under the shroud of unhappiness I was experiencing, I turned to women, and I was not disappointed. I discovered that when we look, we can uncover legions of wonder women who have something important to teach us. The more I learned, the more I felt inspired to share these lessons and messages with others like myself, who were struggling. In the midst of this great unlock, I started an organization called Healthy Women Leaders.

Healthy Women Leaders is a global community that holds space to highlight people and ideas that champion healthy living and radical self-care as a critical means to thrive in a chaotic world. It's a concept, a brand, and a personal passion of mine. The idea for *The Well Within* was born out of the research, interviews, talks, and events I have done for the Healthy Women Leaders' group.

A NOTE ABOUT GENDER

One of the best parts about running Healthy Women Leaders is the incredible women it puts me in front of. For the rest of my life, I will keep my arms wide open to welcome stories and teachings of go-get-em girls from all walks of life. I love highlighting their expertise and drawing the community's attention to the great work they do. Of this, I am 100 percent certain: Women need other women. I am proud to create a forum that encourages new connections and friendships, both personal and professional.

Although some issues that dropped me into my personal darkness are specific to women, or people who identify as she/her, and much of the information I have picked up over the years is from women, the life lessons that I used to better myself can be applied to anyone, regardless of gender. So, if you are a man or a transgender and nonbinary person, I want to welcome you personally to both *The Well Within* and our Healthy Women Leaders community. Though your societal struggles may differ from mine, the roadmap that I lay out from here is intended to be used by you—as a human being in equality.

HOW TO USE
THIS BOOK

I'VE DIVIDED *The Well Within* into five sections of high-level, top-down, big life lessons. These categories are distilled from my years of research and personal experience. I have been living these lessons for a long time now, defining and refining them along the way. Some days I'm more successful at healthy living than others, but overall, these are the practices and concepts I consider as a critical means to keeping my life train steadily on its tracks while maintaining my peace of mind.

Throughout *The Well Within*, you will encounter "truth bombs." These truth bombs are smaller pops of information that can help guide you through daily life. I come back to them frequently. Sometimes I remember them in the heat of the moment, sometimes they whisper to me in my meditation. They are never far away. Think of them as a set of guideposts and mile markers that can help steer you toward a flourishing life.

There are many downloadable resources that can be found on healthywomenleaders.com, including a Whole Life Self-Assessment that I recommend you take before you continue reading. The self-assessment is a great way to benchmark where you are at the beginning of this journey. I also recommend you use this as a check-in mechanism as you proceed, whenever you feel it necessary. And most certainly, take this self-assessment again when you have finished the book, so you can see how far you've come.

In *The Well Within*, we will explore ways to keep yourself physically, mentally, and emotionally healthy. It doesn't need to be done through huge, life-altering changes. You can receive significant benefits from making a series of small, subtle adjustments. And when it seems impossible to stay healthy, when reality hits hard, and you get knocked down a few levels, we'll also look at ways you can intentionally self-heal.

Above all else, this book is designed to offer you the encouragement and permission to go within. It will challenge you to step outside of your comfort zone of perceived safety. It will encourage you to embark on a journey to discover who you are at your core.

When you truly know yourself, by knowing who you are and what you desire, you will be able to craft the life you want to live. You will learn how to set personally inspiring and exciting goals and go after them. You will become one of the people who are awake in the world, who magnetize goodness and opportunity. You will learn how to see, with bright eyes and a clear heart, that despite what we hear on the news, this life is bursting with pure potential that is right here, right now, just waiting for you to claim it.

As you read the five key life lessons that follow, I congratulate you for taking intentional steps on your personal journey. As both the potter and the clay, you have the power to shape this life into whatever you most desire.

THE FIVE KEY LIFE LESSONS

"You've always had the power, my dear,
you just had to learn it for yourself."

—Glinda, the Good Witch, *The Wizard of Oz*

LIFE LESSON 1:
Truly Know Yourself

"It is only when we can truly see what lies within that we can begin to head in the direction of health. This is the domain of the brave and passionate who will not deny the call of goodness that they hear within." [2]

—Erik Stensland, nature and landscape photographer, fellow Coloradan, and astute guy

WHEN I WAS IN COLLEGE, I smoked *far* more marijuana than I should have. I know you are likely thinking, yeah right, so did I, cause . . . well . . . it was college. But I'm not talking about the entire four-year period. I'm talking about an isolated period of time when the two closest people to me, my best friend and my boyfriend, were heavy influences in my day-to-day life. They both *loved* to get high. Like a "blunts-for-breakfast" kind of high. They were blitzed morning, noon, and night, and little lightweight me did all I could to keep up.

It took me a few months of wandering through life in a dazed fog before I realized that this level of MJ consumption was not in *my* best interest. While my friends were happily high, giggling at inside jokes and exploring the nuances of the flowers on our campus, I was trailing along with darting eyes, feeling anxious and missing my clear head.

When the brain fog became too much, I started experimenting with pot detoxes. First, for only a morning, then a day, then a week, then longer. Though it did feel like a separator between my crew and me, my clarity returned and my lust for life started to shine again.

This became a valuable life lesson for me in knowing myself. Just because something works for others does not mean it will work for me. But without knowing what works best for me, how could I possibly create the conditions that would set me up for success? We are all driving different bodies, which have vastly different needs.

Fast-forward to today when I've established a good working relationship with marijuana. MJ and I can comfortably hang out when I don't need to be *on*, when having my inner sparkle is not needed.

I can usually enjoy a high when I'm going to watch a trippy movie, when it's sexy time with my husband, when I want to go internally deep, get super creative, or unlock something within myself. I've learned to *never* get high before going out to talk to people or when I need to problem solve on a practical level. That's how it works for me. To get to this point, I had to learn who I was and what was in my best interest. I needed to discover what was authentic to me.

This is essential for each and every one of us. We must understand who we are and learn what we need, away from all outside influences. To do this, and to achieve any sort of lasting personal growth, we first must become self-aware by going on a quest to *know* ourselves. Maya Angelou says: "Do the best you can until you know better. And then when you know better, do better." This is the "knowing better" part of your journey, and it takes bravery and passion to dive into the well within.

You are the most interesting being in your whole world, and I'm encouraging you to get curious about who this amazing being is and what makes you tick. Are you keeping track of what does or doesn't work for you? Your goal is to gain clarity and authenticity about yourself. But where do you begin?

Imagine yourself standing in the middle of a bustling New York City intersection, with people rushing around you. Everyone has an agenda and some place to be. If you are not intentional about where you are heading, you'll get pushed by the crowd and end up wherever they are going.

Truth Bomb:

Knowing what you *don't* need is just as valuable as knowing what you *do* need.

Human nature comes pre-programmed with an interesting feature—the negativity bias. The negativity bias is the phenomenon that the negative events you experience make a far greater impact on your psychological state than neutral or positive events. Instead of allowing your inner Karen to vehemently share all those negative impressions with everyone near you in Target, why not use the negativity bias in a more productive way? Make note of what you don't like and get curious to fully understand why it rubs you the wrong way. Then look on the other side—what you do like and why. Both are important pieces of understanding YOU. Knowing yourself is a critical first step on your journey within.

The same is true when you are crafting your life. Without intention and direction, you won't end up in the right place for you; you'll end up where you were pushed. But how do you first uncover what it is that you want?

The good news is that you come with a ready-made internal guidance system: intuition. A lovely, beneficial, made-just-for-you inner voice that is always ready to help you make decisions and answer questions with your best interest in mind.

The bad news is that we live in a veritable circus of available distractions that make hearing that inner voice extremely difficult. Being able to turn off or tune out those distractions is imperative, but also really freakin' hard. Learning this is your first task, and if you are not used to it, it can be a doozy.

In this section, we will explore some practical ways in which you can begin to truly get to know yourself and why this may be the most important mission of your life.

Chapter 1:

THE POWER OF
THE PAUSE

THE FIRST FEW TIMES I TRIED to meditate, the experience was an ugly mess. With a mental picture of a serene woman peacefully sitting in the dappled light of a lovely forest, I grabbed a pillow and sat down with my back against my bedroom wall. At this point in my journey, I had heard about meditation from so many sources, it was finally time to give it a go.

It didn't go well. In less than a minute, my mind was racing. I couldn't sit still. I obsessed about how bad I was at this. A light panic crept toward me. A few minutes later, I began to cry, which quickly escalated from a few silent tears into a full-on racking and gasping fit. I rolled off the pillow and took myself to the bathroom, where I blew my nose and wondered how just sitting there with myself with no distractions could have created such an outburst.

Looking in the mirror, the face reflecting back at me was anything but serene. I don't mean to brag, but I have an *epic* post-cry face. I get huge red splotches on my skin; my eyes go red-rimmed and puffy and somehow are able to stay like that for hours. I am the girl who wears the "I've just been crying" look loud and proud for a *long* time post-breakdown. This was the face that was looking back at me. I chucked the whole experience into the "complete fail" category and went about the rest of my day.

Thankfully, this is not where my meditation journey ended. In my research on happiness and thriving, meditation showed up again and again—not only in a spiritual concept without scientific backing. Meditation is now a scientifically studied and proven practice that offers numerous substantial benefits.

Searching on Google Scholar will turn up almost 700,000 research documents related to the benefits of meditation, among them MRI imaging studies that show increased activity in brain regions associated with attention, a higher volume of gray matter, and lessened amygdala response to emotional stimuli. In more practical terms, you will find laundry lists of meditation's many physical and mental health advantages.

Truth Bomb:

It takes bravery to sit with yourself.

Most of us have spent a lifetime looking for reasons and answers outside ourselves. We experience daily life with monumental amounts of distractions. Turning your focus around to look inside yourself, without any filter, is a massive paradigm shift. You have to be brave to sit alone and endure what comes up. It will get more comfortable over time, but like any practice, it must be approached with a long-game perspective. There are no quick fixes or shortcuts when it comes to inner work.

In *The Science of Meditation* video published by The Aspen Institute,[3] the tangible, science-based benefits to meditators include:

* Decreased body pain
* Better immune function
* Less anxiety and depression
* A heightened sense of well-being
* Greater happiness and emotional self-control

This short list alone sounded pretty sweet to me, so I tried again. And again. And again. If I had to cry, I did. I let the tears flow, and I kept at it. As I learned long ago with physical fitness, getting the results you want takes time and practice. Within a few months of regular meditation, the benefits that I was after finally started to appear. I began to feel:

* **Less emotional buy-in to arguments or conflicts.** Instead of getting triggered by comments and having a knee-jerk reaction, I was able to maintain a better sense of the whole discussion. I became more invested in figuring out a resolution than I did in being "right."
* **Less likely to snap at my kids.** Meditation increased both my ability to pause before reacting and my ability to flex into empathy, keeping in mind where they were coming from versus getting 100 percent stuck on my position.
* **Less road rage.** Instead of sending hate lasers at people who pissed me off while driving, I saw them as the same as me—people who were simply driving their cars, though some more politely than others, and going about their day.

* **Better able to experience my senses.** To take a conscious breath, pause and reflect, stop and smell a flower, marvel at the beauty of a bug or a bird.

* **Better connection to myself.** I started to feel more in tune with myself, with a greater understanding of where I was at any given moment. If I felt something extra, I was able to stop and ask myself why.

In short, meditation gives me more say in my reaction to a situation. It provides a cushion of space between what happens to me and how I choose to respond. I am able to more objectively see situations for what they are from a higher level versus getting caught up and playing my role as a participant in that situation.

The number of sessions per week and specific length of time for each session is a personal choice. I started a few times a week for about ten minutes. I now meditate almost every morning for fifteen to thirty minutes. Whatever feels right for you *is* right for you, though I cannot stress enough that you have to stick with it to feel the real benefits.

TRY THIS

Your first challenge is to practice becoming still and quiet. This can be done through meditation or by carving out some alone time for yourself. Literally book it on your calendar, if that's what works best for you. Prevent work and family distractions as best you can; turn off your alerts and just be with yourself.

Notice your breathing, in and out. When you have sufficiently stilled yourself, get curious about how you are doing internally. Ask: How am I feeling right now? What does my body feel like? Am

I feeling good or is something off? If something is off, why is that? Have a journal nearby and be prepared to write down whatever comes up. Don't judge it or analyze it too deeply. Let it flow and see what happens.

When you feel like you've "finished," make sure you take a moment to appreciate yourself consciously for doing this, even if it feels bumpy or awkward. Meditation is a practice, and it takes time to feel the flow. Let me tell you from personal experience: it is *so worth it*.

If you are committed to uncovering a more peaceful and present way to live, you'll figure out your way through your meditation. If you are not fully committed, you'll abandon it, and that's okay too. It means that you are not ready yet to stay the course. I do believe you'll find your way back when the timing is right for you. Until then, be gentle with yourself and stay open for the next time you feel the pull to the pause.

WHY

Becoming still and quiet and adopting a meditative practice will afford you a new level of clarity about who you are and why you do what you do. Becoming committed to this practice is the quickest way to the truths within yourself that are waiting to be revealed. This foundational practice will prepare you as you begin to do the deep work.

Chapter 2:
LEARN TO LISTEN
TO YOURSELF

AS HUMANS WE THINK we are alone, the only ones living inside our head, but all of us have a mental inner dialogue that is almost constantly running. When I started soul searching, for the first time in my life, I began to listen more deeply to what was playing up there. It's fascinating, honestly. That inner play-by-play can take on a number of different tones and perspectives.

The main "inner voice" that runs is usually the relatively easy-going, steady commentary that narrates our daily happenings, wants, feelings, and responses. In addition to it, there is also a louder voice, capable of commanding our undivided attention. This voice gives us emotional, heat-of-the-moment commands like "You're done here—quit this job *now!*" or "How could she cut me off like that!?" or "Ugh, I hate you when you are like this!" or, in the heat of a passionate

THE *Well* WITHIN

moment, "OMG, I think I *love you*!" Despite the tone and vigor with which it communicates, this voice is *not* to be trusted.

The voice to be trusted is a separate, distinct one that is much quieter. And because it does not speak with such ferocity, it's far more difficult to hear. This quieter voice is delivered directly from your intuitive guidance within, and it speaks in a language best understood by the heart.

THE INNER GUIDANCE

My inner guidance system is like a calm kindergarten teacher. When she first wants my attention, she asks quietly. She doesn't demand or shout. Nor does she flick the lights or clap her hands or recite some sing-song ditty to get my attention. She is patient and seems almost unconcerned if I don't hear her quiet, but highly important, directions. She'll wait. Although she can be difficult to hear, when I am able to tune into the frequency with which she speaks, I know I need to follow her advice, and I know I won't be led astray. This inner guidance comes from a place of high-vibe energy full of care and support: my intuition.

I am certain you can identify that voice within yourself. Here are some examples:

* *"I think we're done here,"* it will say in a quiet moment of consideration about a lover.
* *"Why couldn't you do this too?"* it implores as you sit in a dark theater, listening to a fantastic keynote speaker who holds the audience in the palm of her hand.
* *"This isn't serving you,"* it says as you get internally riled up over a friend's political nonsense.

36

Truth Bomb:

The voices from within are not created equal.

Inside your mind, you have an inner critic. Inside your heart, you have an inner guide. Both want to help you navigate life, but they are not created equal. The inner critic wants to keep you safe. The inner guide wants to see you grow and thrive. Take time to listen and consider what suggestions you get and where they come from. This is a critical distinction that will help you process the direction you receive from within.

Your inner guide can "speak" to you in many personal-to-you ways. My inner guidance system relays messages to me through feelings, deep knowing, or actual, audible words.

Feelings/Deep Knowing: I often experience a deep knowing or understanding inside of my body. This can happen through a gut reaction—either positive, indicating *yes,* or negative, indicating *no*—in response to meeting a new person, witnessing an event, thinking about an experience, or hearing or reading about recent occurrences. This is when a stimulus, often an external stimulus, elicits an internal response.

* Positive/favorable reactions can feel like clarity, peace, warmth, happiness, joy, excitement, or enthusiasm. These all indicate a general feeling of *yes, do it,* or *good.*
* Negative/unfavorable reactions can feel like unrest, unease, light anxiety, uncomfortableness, or minor physical yuckiness. These are all indications of a feeling of *no* or *don't do it* or *bad.*

Words: Less often, but much more powerful, is when I hear an audible queue or direction inside my mind. This is an actual phrase or sentence that rings through me and is undeniable and unforgettable. One of the most specific times I hear words is before a big speech or presentation when I am in the throes of nervous energy, which tells me to believe in myself above all else.

People can get their inner direction in many ways, so it's important to understand how your intuition speaks specifically to you.

THE INNER CRITIC

The beneficial, guiding messages shared from your intuition are not to be confused with your inner critic. This inner critic is based on "what if" fears about negative situations that could happen. They come from a place of low-vibe energy full of negatives, worries, and doubts.

The inner critic is fond of rehashing every time you misspoke and replaying what you could have done better. This is the same voice that keeps laundry lists of everything you *should* be doing. This voice tries incessantly to protect you by keeping you aware of the zillion ways you could get hurt. This voice is not to be trusted, as its primary goal is to keep you safe from failure or rejection that could *potentially* happen. In theory, this affords you some level of protection against possible threats, but in reality, it holds you back by stifling new experiences and growth.

I'm certain you have heard this voice within yourself. Here are some examples of how an inner critic talks:

* *"You don't know how to do this,"* it reminds you when you consider taking on a new project or stretch assignment at work.
* *"This is probably not going to work out well,"* it says when you amp yourself up for a visit with the family or a date with someone new.
* *"Woah, that looks super dangerous,"* it chides as you consider a zip-lining/sailing/backpacking/insert-whatever-activity-here excursion with a friend.

Understanding that the inner critic is trying to protect you is important. Understanding that you don't need to listen to it is even more important. Instead, pay close attention to the quieter, gentle, loving voice whose guidance is designed to help you further your development, overcome your personal blockers, and reach your higher potential. That is the voice you want to highlight and honor. It is the voice that should get the prime-time spot on the station in your head.

TRY THIS

The first step to take when trying to tune into your inner guidance is to reduce competing noises. Literal noises, like the radio in your car, the TV, alerts on your phone, or the constant yapping of the Debbie Downer in the cube next to you, who just *loves* to fill you up with her issues.

The next step is to practice the pause that we looked at in the previous chapter, inviting in stillness and quiet that creates space for your inner guidance to become more understandable.

The **body scan** is another practice that can help you connect with your inner guidance. It is a somatic exercise that allows you to check in with your physical self. After you've become still, start at either the top of your head or the tips of your toes and mentally scan through each part of your body. Direct your awareness inside, allowing you to reconnect intentionally with your physical self. Don't judge or critique what you feel; simply bring gentle awareness to each section of your body, noting what feels good and healthy as you relax and release what is tense or tight. Send love to any body parts that hurt. This practice will bring you back home into your body and will better prepare you to be able to hear your inner guidance.

Get into the habit of recording whatever guidance you receive. This guidance may be delivered in the form of feelings, words, or intuitive hits. Whether the guidance comes during quiet moments or periodically throughout your day, take note of the messages you receive. Even if you don't understand their meaning, write them down in a journal so you can reference the information later. As time goes on, you will get more comfortable with this practice of inner listening, and the guidance you receive will become easier to distill.

WHY

When you can hear the wisdom of your inner guidance, you will be better able to navigate daily life with more clarity and authenticity. When you are stuck in indecision or unsure of what to do next, you will have an intuitive navigation system to turn to. Over time, you will come to see this as a reliable source of actionable information. Moreover, learning not to pay attention to the negative, inner critic voice will help you live more peacefully on a day-to-day basis.

Chapter 3:
WHAT'S WITHIN YOUR CONTROL?

WHEN MY SON WAS THIRTEEN, he talked about moving away from home. We lived in Colorado, but we've got a critical mass of family in Florida, and over the next two years, he became increasingly vocal about his desire to move back to the East Coast, where his father lives.

My husband, who's been my son's stepfather since he was four, and I met in Florida. After living there for many years, we were ready for a change. When we moved west, it was intentional. We settled in the foothills of the Rocky Mountains, and a day didn't pass without me feeling a profound sense of gratitude that we lived in such a beautiful location. It became increasingly apparent that my son was not going to change his mind, and my peace and happiness began to erode as his requests escalated.

Rather than allow what had become painfully clear *was* happening *to* happen, I decided instead to move the whole family from our place of peace and happiness to a place where we didn't want to be. At that time, my mama bear heart couldn't face the reality of my kids not being together. It was incomprehensible that I would live so far from my firstborn. To make matters worse, the COVID-forced lockdown had us fiercely missing our extended family.

Whatever the concoction of causes, the effect was in motion. We made the decision to leave and regretted every single step along the way. I cried each day as we packed up the house. I drove in a dazed stupor across the country, leaving my home to go to a place where I knew deep down I didn't want to be. When we arrived, it was a continuation of the same feelings—feeling out of place, unhappy, and missing the *true* home we had regretfully left.

We experienced what it's like when we resist what we know is true. It was messy and uncomfortable, and unless we were prepared to resign ourselves to a situation that didn't fit—which we weren't, it would never work. Our health and happiness declined sharply, our stress went through the roof, and none of us, except for my son, were happy. I had to face the truth—that even though this was right for my son, we were never meant to be there. We lasted ten months before throwing in the beach towel and moving back to our happy place.

Life can—and will—surprise you in an unlimited number of ways. Getting laid off from your job. Finding out you are pregnant. Your relationship, the one that you bet the house on, falls apart. An illness is diagnosed. A death occurs in your family. Your adult child moves back home. You get in an accident. The other guy wins the election. You get your dream job offer, but it's for a company on the other side of the country.

Some life changes are remarkable, some are horrible, and most fall somewhere in between. The only guarantee we have is that life will change, and despite our best efforts, we will not be able to force it to go our way. There is a huge lesson in this, one that is absolutely crucial to overall happiness: we have to learn when to go with the flow and when to work hard to create change.

Resisting is when you know something is happening—you can feel it as a truth in your gut and see signs of it all around you—but as I did, you firmly refuse to believe that it's going down like this. You do whatever you can to fight the flow. I knew my son was moving away from home, but I couldn't bear the thought of the reality that would create. So, I fought the flow and moved my whole family across the country in a futile attempt to remedy something that was already destined to occur.

Allowing is entering the peaceful state in which you take the queues from the Universe and let yourself be led because you have a healthy dose of trust that this is the way it needs to be. You may not like or agree with what's happening, but you trust that you are being led in the right direction. Perhaps toward learning a new truth. Toward having a new experience. Toward the next right step in your journey. Whether it works out the way you wanted or not, you know that the way it happens is indeed the way it's supposed to be.

Truth Bomb:

Resisting is painful, allowing is freeing, surrendering is magical.

Despite how much we toil and try, we actually don't have control over much in our world. The one aspect of life we do have control over is our reactions to the situations we find ourselves in. There are three emotional positions you can take. **Resisting** what you know to be true (ouch). **Allowing** events to unfold by releasing your white-knuckled grip on the outcome that you want (way better). **Surrendering** your emotional angst with a heaping dose of trust that things will work out exactly as they should (ahh). Learning to practice a "thoughtful response" instead of an "impulsive reaction" is key to staying even-keel in an out-of-your-control world.

There is a big difference between allowing and being passive or sitting idly by when you know that something is not right for you. In my case, I could have allowed my son to go to Florida, as that is what all the signs were pointing toward. However, when it became undeniably clear that Florida was the wrong place for me to live, staying there would have been an example of being passive—and miserable.

Sitting idly by when something is deeply wrong for you—be it a lover, a job, drinking too much, or where you live, for example—is sure to erode your well-being. As soon as you sense that what is happening feels "off" in significant ways, do whatever you can to make a change that better suits your health and happiness and honors the way you want to live.

Perhaps the most important tool of all in this lesson is knowing when to **surrender.** Surrender is the practice of taking your worries and intentionally releasing them to the Universe. One way to surrender is to experience it through your body.

Begin by physically feeling the weight of what is bothering you, then identify where that shows up in your body. Next, imagine removing that weight, physically decoupling it from your body and sending it out to the Universe. You must be fully committed to releasing yourself from that pain and moving on, no matter what may come next. When you embody the deep belief that whatever happens next will be right, whether or not it is the outcome you intended, complete release is possible.

You can invoke this powerful tool when you have exhausted your brain and recognize that certain events or circumstances are not in your control. This is tough, deep work, but the reward you'll receive is a huge sense of freedom and peace, which is well worth the emotional output necessary to get there.

In my case, I could have surrendered rather than resisted when plagued with the internal struggle that I didn't want my son to leave. At the time, although I could sense what needed to happen for him, I wasn't capable of trusting the Universe with such an enormous emotional decision. Sometimes, though, the only way to arrive at a true place of surrender is to experience the failure of your white-knuckled grip on control or to witness the situation get even worse than it was before. We live, and we learn. I learned from this one, and I now use this powerful practice anytime I am faced with a dilemma, despite the size or severity of the situation.

TRY THIS

Time for a gut check: Are you a controller? Think about your most recent experiences that felt bumpy or less than smooth. Were you trying to control someone else's behavior or how they felt? Were you trying to control situations or outcomes that you couldn't possibly affect? Take time to consider this and write about it in your journal.

* Think of a time when you *resisted* a situation and detail what happened.
* Think of a time when you *allowed* a situation and detail what happened.
* Finally, think of a time when you fully *surrendered* and detail what occurred.
* How did you feel in each situation? What did you learn along the way?

WHY

A quote from the 14th Dalai Lama that I always reference when I catch myself grappling with control in an uncomfortable situation is: "If a problem is fixable, if a situation is such that you can do something about it, then there is no need to worry. If it's not fixable, then there is no help in worrying. There is no benefit in worrying whatsoever."[4]

To sum it up, if you can do something about a situation that is bothering you, do it. If you can't, then let it go. Either way, don't spend too long worrying about it. Remember: you *always* have control over your response to a situation, and a thoughtful response is better than an emotional reaction any day. The key here is to identify if you do or do not have control over the situation.

Eyes wide open, my friend. This is about flowing with, not against, the ebbs and flows of daily life. Relinquishing your controlling grip on uncontrollable situations is the golden ticket that will free you from wasting heaps of time and effort.

LIFE LESSON 2:
Watch What You Take On and In

"No is a necessary magic. No draws a circle around you with chalk and says 'I have given enough.'" [5]

—Feminist poet and astute observer McKayla Robbin, author of *We Carry the Sky*

IMAGINE, IF YOU WILL, a beautiful blank canvas. This canvas sits in a public space, say, a city square. A table beside the canvas holds a selection of brushes and paints that are available for the passersby to add their mark. Some people make beautiful, elaborate, detailed strokes, while others splash the paint dramatically. Some add stickers, others use spray paint, and others who are not having such a good day might take a sharpie and write profanity. In the course of one day, that pristine blank canvas has turned into a mess of everyone's various marks.

You, my dear friend, are that canvas. Each day you can start out fresh and new, and each day, if left unguarded, you will get filled up by the marks of everyone who happens to pass you by. If they are happy and well balanced, you will take on beautiful marks and inspirational sentiments that can lift you up and motivate you. On the other hand, if those who pass you by are unhappy, violent, angry, or otherwise malaligned, you can get splashed with a veritable shit-storm of negative messaging.

We human beings, as you may have noticed, are social animals. We revolve around one another almost constantly. If you leave your-self open to it, you will pick up impressions from the people you come into contact with. This can be a generally good experience if you've cultivated a key group of inspirational people. But this can become a bad situation if you haven't.

These canvases of ours are subject to far more than just the atti-tudes of the people around us. Our minds and bodies can take on a whole lot more. Consider the social media messages that we absorb all day long. Or the news and the vehement opinions of polarized political groups. Or the environmental toxins that our physical bodies are exposed to. And what about the toxins we choose, like drugs, alcohol, jealousy, and gossip?

As we go through this section, a crucial key is the word, concept, and potency of "no."

To protect ourselves in this wild world, we need to become aware of what we take on and in. We need to be able to say no to the things that don't serve us.

In the following chapters, we will look at what we take into our bodies, minds, and home environments and how that affects us. We will learn what it takes to clear the clutter from those spaces. Our goal here is to reclaim our blank canvases and protect them, so they get filled up with only what we decide is worthy of making a mark.

Truth Bomb:

No is one of the most powerful tools in your personal arsenal.

Oh my goodness, the power of the beautiful "no." The one tiny word that can so quickly and effectively prevent you from heading down, or going further along, the wrong path. The word that can shut a door before it even has a chance to open. Embrace the word "no." Learn how to feel comfortable saying it without apologies. Own it! Dole it out as needed and stick by it.

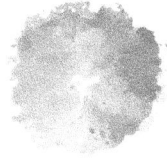

Chapter 4:
WHAT ARE YOU CONSUMING PHYSICALLY?

WHEN WE TALK ABOUT what you *should* and *should not* consume, I cannot stress enough that this is unique for each person. To help illustrate this point, allow me to introduce the concept of the Earth Suit. The Earth Suit is the body you are wearing as you move through life. It's akin to a vehicle that takes you everywhere you need to go, from birth to death and all the places in between. It's what we have to feed, water, bathe, and care for as we move about our days on this planet. It's what gives us great physical pleasures, and it's what begins to break down as we age. No two Earth Suits are alike, and the closer you get to other people, the clearer this becomes. Allow me to share some examples of the differences between my husband's Earth Suit and my own.

Sleeping: My Earth Suit likes to get up early in the mornings. I wake up around five a.m. each day, feeling more or less fresh and energized. I regularly take a short afternoon nap. I tend to fall asleep pretty early as well, around nine p.m. or so. My husband's Earth Suit operates on a far different schedule. He wakes up a couple of hours later than me, he stays up a couple of hours later than me, and he almost never takes an afternoon nap.

Fun marital point one: Having me as your movie-watching partner at night is *not* super interesting, as I'm almost always going to end up bobbleheading and open-mouth drooling my way to an early bedtime long before the credits.

Eating: Let's look at what we feed the Earth Suit. I like to graze all day long. I've worn a figurative path on the floor from my office to the kitchen. I like small meals often throughout the day, with lots of veggies and not much meat. My husband can go half the day without eating. In fact, he often fasts or chooses to have only two meals a day. He loves red meat and doesn't complain if there isn't anything green on his plate.

Fun marital point two: My husband has legendary BBQ skills and really enjoys long-smoking big salty hunks of red meat. I've recently cut way back on my meat intake, and sadly, this means he loses his meat-eating partner.

Substances: How about alcohol or drugs? I tend to have a cocktail or two in the evenings. My husband prefers to skip it or just have one. Any more than that and he gets a headache—and it's likely lights out early. The same amount of caffeine that helps put a pep in my step will rocket him through the roof and ensure he's a jittery mess for all his calls that day.

It's fascinating stuff, these Earth Suits of ours. For example, one person can have a couple of drinks socially, but for another person, that would make them feel like an alcoholic. One person needs a 30-mg THC chocolate bar to catch a good high, while another person (me again) needs a 5-mg chill pill to get nice and lifted. Two people can eat almost the same foods, yet one is borderline obese. One person can run a marathon, and the other person will struggle through a short run.

I'm sure you have people you know who are driving far different models of the Earth Suit than yours. Every Earth Suit is different, so the key is finding the perfect blend for *yourself* that helps you achieve your physical goals and feel your personal best.

TREATING THE BODY RESPECTFULLY

If this body is your vehicle to get through life, wouldn't you want to drive the best model possible? The one that can go far and fast, the one with all the bells and whistles? Even if the luck of the draw didn't deal you the Ferrari you wanted, but instead, you got a super solid, well-built, and trusted sedan, that isn't *that bad*, right? The trick is, though, you've gotta keep it filled up with gas, make sure it's maintained, and treat it with a certain amount of care for it to continue running well.

Truth Bomb:

Treat your one and only Earth Suit with great respect.

We have been gifted with this one perfectly imperfect body. Fighting with it, disrespecting it, talking shit about it, poisoning it, or otherwise destroying it is just *gunking up* the only vehicle you have to carry you through life. I firmly believe that we should all treat our personal Earth Suits with great care and respect. This does not mean that you should deny yourself what you want or love that is less than healthy. Indulges are key—in moderation. As long as you are able to regulate your indulgences so you are in control of them instead of them being in control of you, have at it! I sure do.

Indulgences aside, let's talk about the daily stuff we put into these bodies. Take a moment now and ask yourself:

* How is the quality of the food I eat?
* Do I maintain a balanced diet?
* Am I prioritizing natural foods from the earth?
* How much of what I eat is chemically infused and processed?
* Do I drink plenty of clean water?
* How is my consumption of sugar, caffeine, alcohol, and drugs? Do I practice moderation, or are there areas of concern that need to be addressed?

Periodically asking these questions will help you keep a close eye on your internal barometer, not in a judgmental sort of way, but with a general awareness that will help you spot when something is going awry.

Sometimes it can be difficult for us to see ourselves clearly to understand if we have been overindulging in the unhealthy or not consuming enough of the healthy. If you have some solidly supportive folks in your court, take note when a few of them offer the same or similar observations. I've found when multiple trusted people in my life make the same comments at the same time, I need to take notice.

If you find yourself more dependent on a food, beverage, or substance than you would like to be, that is your cue that it's time for a bigger change. Though it may not feel like it now, you are not as helpless or as beholden to "the way things are" as you might think. But, most likely, you will need to lean in and flex into a new level of effort to make this a long-lasting change. Try adopting "self-empowerment through self-discipline" as your new motto for a period of time. Going further into details about this approach is out of the scope of this book, but there are many other incredibly helpful resources that are available on this topic.

Additionally, if you feel like you want a change but need help decoupling yourself from whatever substance isn't making you feel good, I implore you to seek professional help.

TRY THIS

It can be helpful to keep a journal of what's going into your body. You can start small by tracking what you eat in a day. Then add in how you feel at specific intervals during the day—for instance, in the morning, at noon, and at night. Next, take a look at what you've consumed during those particular times of the day and see if you can make a correlation between your physical or mental sentiments at those times. If this works for you, try to track a full week. At the end of the week, see if you can spot patterns. What makes you feel good? What makes you feel gross? Identify what needs to change based on how you felt.

WHY

The goal is to feel great in your body, and the key is to be brave enough to make whatever changes are necessary to accomplish that goal. When you unlock the fact that feeling good in your body is the foundation for feeling good in your life, you will be that much closer to truly thriving.

Chapter 5:
WHAT ARE YOU CONSUMING MENTALLY?

ONE OF MY MOST COMMON STRUGGLES these days is around how much I use my phone. This ebbs and flows for me, but if left unchecked, I can easily get lost in the oblivion of the infinite scroll.

My digital drugs of choice are Instagram, TikTok, YouTube Shorts, and, most regrettably, the news. I tend to find these little bite-sized video clips and headlines irresistible, scrolling from one to the next in an automatic, zombie-like fashion, with only a micro-emotional reaction here or there. Sometimes, it's a slight grimace for something unpleasant, or a little out breath for something funny, or a pause over something interesting or disturbing. The gestures barely acknowledge that I've just exposed myself to input that could have a significant impact on my mind. When I catch myself doing this, I wonder: What am I searching for, anyway?

I try to keep this away from family time, but man, watching baseball is boring enough that sometimes the phone seems to fall into my hand when my husband is in his happy zone on the couch beside me. And then there are the times when I need a mental break from playing dolls with my daughter and I start scrolling. Doing this in front of my daughter hurts me the most because when I look up, I see two beautiful brown eyes staring at me. Even worse is to consider that as she continues to get older, those beautiful brown eyes will be staring down at whatever nonsense I'm watching.

I find that the more I use my phone, the more adrift I feel. I'm well aware that this is a waste of precious time, but the struggle is real. There are even times when I find something inspiring as I scroll, something that should be given more thought or written down in a journal. But when I'm doomscrolling, I struggle to make myself stop. The invisible pull of finding that *next thing* is just too strong. I scroll, I swipe, I go into some sort of mindless stupor. And I know for a fact that I'm not alone.

Truth Bomb:

The phone is a fantastic tool to decouple you from the present moment.

We are the generations who are serving as the guinea pigs for smartphones. Every day, we carry around a digital distraction device right on our person. We keep it an arm's reach away when we sleep. This *thing* is always with us, and my god, does it get our attention. We know the benefits of having a supercomputer in our pocket, but the drawbacks are now starting to come to light too. There are widespread reports of digital addiction, increased feelings of social isolation, anxiety, and depression. It's clear that these devices are not healthy for us with unregulated use, but as with any new and repeatedly used product, it takes time for the real issues to become apparent. In the meantime, *reduce your smartphone use* and get some of your brainpower back.

DIGITAL CONSUMPTION

In a July 21, 2023, article on Reviews.org,[6] troubling facts highlight the average American's relationship with their cell phone, including the following:

* Fifty-seven percent report that they are addicted to their cell phone
* Checks their phone 144 times per day
* Spends four hours, twenty-five minutes each day on their cell phone
* Will spend over two months (sixty-five days) on their phones in 2023

Well, this is pretty horrible. I'm honestly worried about what this means for our human brains and the effects it will have on our culture. I don't want to be part of those stats, and yet, I still feel myself struggling between using the phone as the super tool it is and not spending so much time on my phone that it interrupts my regularly scheduled social functioning.

As I consider what we are looking at when we spend this time on our phones, the behavior can be broken down into a few main categories: always-on work mode, social media mania, marketing messages, negative news, and addictive games. It's no wonder that the more time I spend on my phone, the worse I feel.

Working from the phone: Never being able to shut off work is a huge issue for Americans who have lost their bearings on what work-life balance is.

Relaxing on the phone: Social media posts can be entertaining but also inspire jealousy and feelings of not being good enough. The games that are available are designed to keep you playing, like slot machines or other questionably addictive pastimes that reach up and firmly grab hold of your unsuspecting brain.

Absorbing from the phone: It is estimated that the average person will see about 10,000 digital ads per day. Add to that, commercials from the TV and radio, news articles your parents send you, headlines on news sites, the veritable firehose of happenings on social media, and you are thoroughly and completely saturated with *noise*. Now, even my local gas station has monitors running ads while I fuel up the car. Much of the messaging that we see can be broken down into three main categories:

1. Fear-based, consumption-focused messages: "You are not good enough as you are, so quick, buy this to get/be better." These are advertisements that want you to buy something. Bottom line: Spend, spend, spend!

2. Fear-based, think-like-me messages: "If you don't get on this side of the issue, you will be with the losers, and God help you then." These are divisive societal commentary issues, which are especially popular these days. Bottom line: F you if you're not me!

3. Fear-based, shock-and-awe click-me messages: "To get your eyeballs over here, here's a hot heaping pile of horror that you can't look away from." These are the clickbait titles that highlight some of the more horrible stories around. Bottom line: Too bad about your psyche, I got your view!

LIMITING DIGITAL CONSUMPTION

When I catch myself in a "using the phone too much" phase, I have to make a concentrated effort to get my brain back. To do so, I start by setting up little roadblocks for myself.

If I find that I'm automatically opening up my phone, I challenge myself to answer truthfully: What am I unlocking this for? If the answer is something half-assed, like "checking the weather" or "looking at when that meeting is on Friday," I make myself put it away. I stop taking it into the bathroom with me. I stop using it at red lights. I stop using it at my daughter's gymnastics practice. It's honestly harder than it should be—which is proof of the addictive nature of our digital devices.

When I make a commitment to use the phone less, and with enough of those little challenges accomplished, I start to feel better. Then, I make the challenges even bigger: Don't touch the phone again until after dinner. Long before bedtime, plug it in to charge and leave it there. Over time and with continuous effort, it begins to get easier to disconnect. The FOMO begins to ebb. What's happening around me becomes clearer and more interesting, and I'm better able to focus on that.

Perhaps one of the most obvious actions to take when implementing steps to limit digital consumption is to make adjustments to the phone itself. If you are not yet comfortable removing the addictive apps from the phone completely, try removing them from the home screen. That way, they are not the first items you see when you unlock your device. Keep an eye on the trackers that share how much time you are actually spending on each app. Make use of the digital wind-down features that your phone offers. Set time limits, like no phone from eight p.m. through eight a.m. Set up your device in a way that helps you limit your use.

Aside from freeing up your mental space, an equally big risk in staying focused on your phone is that you miss the important, happening-right-now experiences. Like the smile on your child's face. A yellow butterfly lazily drifting by your window. Your cat doing that cute "flip its head over and look at you" thing. The subtle changes in the colors of the sky at dusk. A shooting star. The dappled pattern of light and shadows against the wall. These are the real moments in life—the tiny, beautiful natural occurrences that are here and gone in an instant. I hate missing these moments, and yet, I still struggle with this always-urging-me-to-pick-it-up device.

Any way you look at it, less is more when it comes to these devices. It would be remiss to ignore that there are many fantastic features these phones provide, giving us access to information, helping keep our kids safe, and abilities that make our lives easier. I don't see a future where we are without our phones, so it's up to us to regulate what we use them for and how much we engage with them.

In my case, I don't want to fill up on nothing. Densely packing my brain space with pointless videos and meaningless news leaves little room for what's important. It keeps me bobbing on the surface of life, searching for some unnamed *thing* and never finding it. Screw that! Phone down.

SOCIAL CONSUMPTION

Moving beyond media, let's consider the messages that you may be exposed to in personal circles. Do you listen to or participate in gossip or other toxic topics of conversation? Do you have family members or "friends" who put you down or dissuade you from your dreams? Your mind is a tool that can be used for greatness, but if it's completely polluted with other people's agendas, how will you ever be able to use it for your own good?

When you start living and operating from a place of personal power, you model healthy, happy, and whole living by example and give the people around you permission to do the same. This will elicit two very distinct reactions from people. One group of people will be drawn to you; they are attracted to the fact that you are out there living your life on your terms in the way that works best for you. They will congratulate you and feed into that high-flying level of greatness. These people will uplift you and leave you feeling inspired, seen, and heard. Awesome! Those people are your tribe.

There will, of course, be another group of people who are threatened by your newfound ability to better yourself. Those people are the haters, the doubters, the ones who fear change, or the ones who are on such a different path that they cannot understand where you are coming from. They might feel threatened by where you are because it highlights where they are *not*. These are not your people, and trying to get them to understand what you are experiencing is a waste of your time.

Embarking upon a personal development journey often means that you will lose people along the way. When you start making positive changes in your life, other people may feel their stagnancy or bad habits become highlighted. What you once shared that used to bind you together may be exactly what you are shedding, and you may not have much in common any longer. This can feel confusing and downright lonely as your life begins to change. The good news is that the more we move toward self-realization, the more we will attract like-minded people who share our values and personal development goals.

Truth Bomb:

Do not waste time or energy on negative people who don't support you.

Check your social circle for people who are on the "misery loves company" path and be aware that they will likely try to pull you down to match where they are. Unless they are open to change, I suggest you avoid those people before they bring you down. If you can't avoid them, limit your time with them. You are not tuned into the same frequency right now, and trying to get them to understand will be pretty much impossible.

REDUCING NEGATIVE SOCIAL INFLUENCES

There are a few groups of people to avoid when you are committed to protecting your mental space. Here are the main groups and a description of each:

Energy Vampires: These are people who suck up your energy and leave you feeling wasted or tired after hanging out or speaking with them. These folks always seem to want to get something from you when you interact, such as your agreement with their side of a situation. They drain you energetically.

Negative Nellies: If people around you are living below their potential, it will be difficult for them to believe that you can reach yours. These people will be thrilled to share their unsolicited opinions as to why things don't or won't work out for you, or for them. This "advice" may be coming from a place of "not wanting you to get hurt." Be careful not to believe or take on what other people think of you—it's actually none of your business.

Also, be careful of that negative voice in your head that we considered in Chapter 2. If you frequently hear a loud inner critic that shares negative commentary on your life, rest assured *that voice* isn't the real you and doesn't need to be taken seriously.

Gossip Queens: These are people who focus their brain space and energy on other people, often as a way to make themselves feel better. They critique, judge, and stamp other people with whatever their outside subjective opinion is. It's easy to fall into this pattern of behavior, but we are remiss if we think we can judge anyone else's life. Each one of our journeys is wholly unique, and we can never truly know what someone else is going through.

It is important to note that there will always be people, including work colleagues, family members, neighbors, and others, who you do not have the option to remove from your life. If having them walk the plank is not an option, limit the time you spend with these people. If you can't limit it sufficiently, then limit the brain space you give them. Make sure you are taking stellar care of yourself from the inside out so their boobery does not affect you in an unadulterated way.

INCREASING POSITIVE SOCIAL INFLUENCES

When it comes to your social circles, amplifying the positive influences around you can be just as important as limiting the negative. Positive influences are the people in your life who are supportive and vocal fans of the person you are and the work you do. They champion your efforts, and you can count on them to stand you up and dust you off when life knocks you down. They inspire you as you inspire them, and you enjoy a reciprocal relationship of accountability and ingenuity.

I am truly blessed to have built up a solid core group of amazing women who are on similar paths as me. We all navigate our lives in a way that we are able to be there for one another when needed. I value their support, advice, inspiration, and friendship immensely.

You don't need too many of these people in your world, but you do need some. If you don't have anyone who fits this description, it's time to seek some out. There are a number of amazing communities linked through common interests that you can join to put yourself in closer contact with like-minded people. It's no big surprise that I also suggest the Healthy Women Leaders community, but there are countless others you can seek out as well. Give yourself bonus points if you find a group in relative geographic proximity because in relationships like these, online-only won't give you the full experience.

TRY THIS

Mentally run through your day and compile a list of the places and ways you are most likely to take in a blast of negative messaging or energy. From there, you can set up boundaries to protect your personal space. To start, what are one or two small measures you can put in place to restrict the flow of undesirable energy toward you?

Here are some ideas:

* Turn off whatever you're listening to before you get out of the car. That way, you can control when you are ready to start taking in information on your next drive instead of finding yourself mindlessly absorbing whatever comes along next.

* Are there people in your life who leave you feeling icky after you interact with them? Can you back off from those interactions or, at the very least, emotionally distance yourself from them? Intentionally spend more time with the people who champion you, lift you up, and inspire you.

* This one is big, but necessary. *I implore you*—do not let your phone be the last thing you look at before bed or what you look at first when you wake up. Give yourself a break from the onslaught of information and, instead, meditate or at least check in with yourself for a few moments before you go to sleep or first engage with your day.

* Bonus: Try to check in with yourself at least once or twice a day when you pick up your phone. Ask yourself, why am I unlocking this? If you can't come up with a real or good reason, put it down and instead find the nearest piece of nature (a houseplant, a slice of blue sky out your window, the fur-baby napping at your feet) and take a moment to experience and appreciate that.

WHY

Watching what you take in mentally is a critical step toward safe-guarding your overall well-being. Your inner mental landscape is incredibly important, and it's downright impossible to think for yourself when you are told what you "should" be thinking or doing much of the time.

When you turn down the volume on the noise that is constantly blasted at you, you will be better able to hear your inner guidance and honor what *you* want. This allows you to keep your mind healthier. No one but you can make that happen, so carve out some brain space for yourself in this overstimulating world. You will be thankful you did.

Chapter 6:
HOW DO YOU FEEL IN YOUR HOME ENVIRONMENT?

IT'S WONDERFUL THAT AFTER many years of dorms and roommates and apartments and townhouses, my family and I are super grateful to live in a beautiful home. We have plenty of space, a lovely design and flow to the house, and hell, we even have a view.

There are moments when I stand peacefully in this house, sipping my coffee in the kitchen, and feel such a rush of gratitude for the gift that it is to have such a lovely, safe space. Yet, there are other moments when I feel like I could hulk-smash the never-ending dishes or set fire to the mountain of laundry that never goes away, no matter how much of it I do.

THE *Well* WITHIN

Despite the great leaps that women have taken toward equality over the years, there are still areas where women tend to experience significant levels of inequality. Perhaps the most obvious area is in the home. This includes housework, childcare, and the "invisible workload" or "mental load" that comes with the management of the home and family. This invisible workload represents keeping track of what needs to happen for the home to run smoothly—think pediatrician appointments, gutter cleanings, and grocery lists—and it costs a great amount of brain space to manage.

It is estimated that in traditional heterosexual relationships, women still spend more than double the amount of time on housework than their husbands (4.6 hours per week for women versus 1.9 hours per week for men) and almost two hours more per week on caregiving, including tending to children.[7] In non-heterosexual relationships, there could also be one partner who is doing more than their share of the work around the house.

This was never more apparent than during the COVID lockdown, when suddenly everyone was home *all the time.* I and many of the women I know quickly went insane as we attempted to keep up with this new thousand-fold level of effort required to keep the homestead running. Instead of making only one or two meals a day, there were now three meals to be planned, shopped for, cooked, and cleaned up afterward. Having people at home continuously meant there was way more to pick up, clean up, and scrub down. Not only were household responsibilities at an all-time high, but we had to manage our children's education as well. The brief mental respite that we, as parents, can feel when our kids are off at school was erased.

To top it off, worry about the state of the worldwide pandemic was paramount. Thankfully, that time has passed, but it was eye-opening and unforgettable for everyone who experienced it.

Whatever the dynamics of your relationship, if you are shouldering more of the workload or not, what can you do to make your homelife easier or more comfortable? That can only be answered after taking an assessment of where you truly stand. So, riddle me this, Batman: How do you feel in your home?

I know very well what it's like to *not* feel peace in your home. In my young adult years, when I was living with a completely unsuitable partner, home was anything but a sanctuary. It was a place to escape from and avoid as much as possible. While this was a terrible way to live, there was a silver lining: it gave me a contrast. I was able to see what I didn't want with an in-my-face clarity that could only be earned from living it, and it helped me make the eventual decision to leave.

If you find yourself in an anti-peaceful home now, or have in the past, as painful as it might be to look at your situation, remember: there is something to be grateful for. You can use this incredibly important "hell no" information to shape the choices you make next that will better reflect what you *do* want. Those unbearable situations can help guide you to make significant life changes for the better.

The struggles I feel now are more superficial than structural—meaning that it's not about living with the wrong people. Most of the time, I feel great in my home. Sometimes, however, I get overwhelmed with the amount of stuff we have. I've come to understand that when my home is clean and cleared of clutter, I generally feel calmer. When I don't feel so great and piles of *things* start to accumulate, the need for a good cleaning becomes apparent.

Truth Bomb:

How you feel in your home sets the stage for how you feel in your life.

It is essential to feel at peace in your home. We spend so much time there that it's imperative that we feel comfortable, safe, and secure, so we always have a place to rest and recharge from the volatility of the outside world. When we feel comfortable and relaxed in our living spaces, we're more likely to be open, communicative, and present with our family members. Even if your personal circumstances do not allow for a peaceful experience in your home right now, can you designate a small corner or other area that can serve as your safe bubble? A peaceful home, or small space within your home, provides steady ground for relaxation and management of stress, two crucial elements for maintaining mental and emotional well-being.

Although I don't have the magic answer to gender inequality and the lopsided division of labor around the home, I do know that there are a number of practical steps that can be taken to help yourself feel better in your own home.

MAKING CHANGES AT HOME
Method 1: Reevaluate the division of labor among everyone inside and outside of the home
Here's a novel idea. Talk to your people about what's going on. Sounds easy enough, but I know for me, this is probably the hardest action to take, especially to have a conversation when I'm not angry. Expressing our feelings in anger is not the right approach.

On the other hand, quietly martyring ourselves to the cause is also not the right approach. I've certainly tried this one too. When you stay quiet and keep your family in the dark about how you are feeling, the work stays on your plate, and all those hours you spend wishing that someone could read your vicious thoughts are just wasted time.

Instead, talk it out from a factual perspective, in an unemotional moment, which is a much better approach. You will be better able to express yourself and allow for an open dialogue.

Another option here is to outsource the help. If you have the means, consider a cleaning service. I've spoken to many women executives who swear that this one service helped their peace of mind, and their relationships, immensely. I can attest to this myself.

Method 2: Clear the clutter and don't buy more things you don't need
In today's world of Amazon Prime-enabled, almost-instant gratification, we can have just about anything we want conveniently

dropped off at our doorstep in a matter of days, if not hours. If left unchecked, that creates the potential for a ton of new stuff to enter your home that will most likely be added to already stuffed closets or junk drawers. Add to that the mountain of papers your children bring home from school that are tough to throw away, along with their toys in every corner of every room.

Look around your home and notice how much of what's there remains untouched or barely noticed—including knickknacks, boxes still unpacked from your last move, and kitchen drawers full of way more stirring spoons than you will ever need. The list goes on and on.

Minimalism and Marie Kondo-style decluttering[8] get a lot of attention these days, and for good reason. Many people are stuck in the habit of near-constant buying. While you don't need to go over the top and throw away 90 percent of what you own, we all should take stock of the state of our homes and begin—or continue—to watch our spending habits. Ask yourself whether you need what you have around you and what you want to buy. Are you filling up your space because you actually require or love the items? If not, why do you keep them? And why are you getting more?

There is so much societal pressure to buy, buy, buy. This costs you money, time, brain space, and physical space in your home. When you see this constant consumption habit for what it really is, you then have a choice if you want to break away from it. This will free up your time and money so you can have deeper experiences and get involved in more beneficial and rewarding activities.

Method 3: Shake things up
If the house is picked up and organized to your liking, but there is still something off, it may be time to consider some outside expertise.

Much in the way that Marie Kondo can help you declutter your home, there are some great methodologies and many inspirational designers that can help you truly make your space your own.

Fêng Shui: Fêng shui is the ancient Chinese art of aligning the items in your home to allow for the free flow of Chi (energy). Fêng shui is the practice of arranging your space to create balance and harmony between an individual and their environment. I'm not an expert on this by any means, but I do know when a house *feels* good. If this sounds interesting to you, there are some amazing experts with books, websites, and social feeds to better teach you this ancient art.

Hygge: Hygge (pronounced Hoo-gah) is the Danish practice of making your home cozy and comfy by way of soft lighting and comfortable fabrics and textures, which creates a general feeling of warmth in your home. When I first learned about Hygge, I began to implement some of the recommendations, just making minor changes around my home. A neighbor who had been in my home often exclaimed one day, "I don't know what you are doing in here, but it feels better every time I come in!" Proof in the practice right there.

User Experience: I've spent most of my career working in digital technology, and one of the core concepts to focus on when creating a website or an application is the user experience. This means being aware of the path people take as they experience your tech and continuously making optimizations to highlight the good and minimize the bad in the user's journey. Why not apply this to your home? What's working in there, and what isn't? Make slight adjustments to help with functionality and flow. For instance, put up a towel rack in the bathroom where you always wish there was one. Put a bowl to hold your keys on the hallway table where you usually drop them. Get a mug holder. Keep your spices closer to where you cook. Put a laundry basket where your kids throw their clothes every day after school.

Another note here is to fix whatever needs fixing. It's easy to create a workaround when something breaks, and over time, you can get into the habit of the workaround. Most likely, it's not as efficient or effective, and maybe not even as safe as it would be to do the repair. Take a good, hard look at what's not working right and make the fixes that need to be made.

Get Some Green: As a recovered plant killer, I am now happy to see my little green babies flourishing all over the house. Turns out, you can't just buy a plant, bring it home, and expect it to thrive. That little guy is alive and requires much of the same care that you do, including water, food, sunlight, and a bigger pot when it gets too large for the one it's in. As soon as I looked at the plants as living beings and not decorations, my black thumb turned green, and they grew.

Get Inspired: Do you know what your style is or what inspires you? Get curious and start researching different home and interior designs. A favorite designer of mine is Justina Blakely of Jungalow.[9] She is an expert at designing colorful spaces that always contain plants. Her social feeds are full of great design ideas and plant care tips. Find out who inspires you, design-wise, and keep the creativity flowing.

Aside from the division of labor and the look and feel of your house, how else might you be able to set up your home to help you feel better?

At the base level, it's pretty obvious that environmental toxins should never be present in your home. Mold, lead paint, or other toxins need to be removed and/or mitigated immediately. If you are a smoker, well shit—I don't even know what to say to you except *stop it now*. You already know that it is slowly killing you and poisoning everyone else around you. If there is an always-nasty litter box, too much garbage, or a bug problem, fix these situations and keep them fixed. Your home should be clean and comfortable for you and the other people who live there.

At a higher level, your space should also reflect who you strive to be. This can happen in two ways:

1. **Remove what stands between you and your goals.** Take away those items from your home that inspire bad habits or derail you from your goals. If you are trying to drink less, don't keep alcohol around. If you are trying to eat healthier, get rid of the junk food. If you want to be more present with your partner, try removing the TV from your bedroom.

2. **Set up your space to help you accomplish your goals.** Look at your goals and look at your home. What can you do to make it easier for you to get after those goals? If you want to incorporate more yoga into your routine, designate a space for your yoga mat to live so there is zero friction to practice when the mood strikes you. Trying to be more creative? Adjust your desk or designate a writing corner or art area so you are comfortable and have no excuses to postpone getting after your goal.

Your home is where you spend most of your time. Taking the extra effort to make it comfortable and supportive will help to keep you on the right track, which is well worth the effort.

TRY THIS

To start feeling better in your home, first, assess what is working for you and what is not.

* Check for excess in what you have and get rid of duplicates or what is otherwise not wanted or needed.

* When hitting Amazon Prime, give yourself a day or so in between the *want* to buy the product and clicking the "place your order" button. Is the want still there after you wait a couple of days? If so, and if you can honestly say it's something you will use or love or enjoy, then go ahead and get it. If not, back away from the checkout button. Clear the cart and move on.

* Notice when something in your home doesn't feel like it works right, either in experience or in function. Make changes where you can.

* Seek out a new designer or resource that inspires you. See if a small bit of that inspiration can be adopted into your home.

* Make sure your home is set up to reduce whatever friction might be standing between you dreaming about your goals and actually accomplishing your goals.

WHY

Taking action to adjust what doesn't feel right in your home can provide significant benefits to your mental health. Strive to make your home into your safe and comfortable space—your peaceful sanctuary from the often chaotic world outside. I believe that when you feel more comfortable in your home, you will also feel more comfortable in your skin. Creating and maintaining a relaxing environment at home is a critical part of living a wholly healthy and happy life.

LIFE LESSON 3:

Watch What You Give Out

"Compassionate action has to start with ourselves. If we are willing to stand fully in our own shoes and never give up on ourselves, then we will be able to put ourselves in the shoes of others and never give up on them."[10]

—Pema Chödrön, Buddhist teacher, author, nun, mother, peaceful warrior, woman with a highly influential voice in contemporary spirituality

A FEW YEARS BACK, on a beautiful fall day in late September, I had a coffee meeting with a potential client. I was feeling *good*. I mean really good. My business was looking up; my family dynamic was healthy and happy; I had been consistent with my meditation and exercise practices. We sat outside at a hip little cafe in Denver and the day was glorious. The fall colors around me looked extra vibrant. I was moved enough by the spectacle of all the "autumn awesome" around me that I felt I had to mention it. I remarked that I was pretty sure the fall colors were more potent than in past years and asked him if he saw it too. He smiled and said, "No. They look the same to me." *Ha!*

On that day, as the leaves drifted down, I was totally rapt in the splendor of it all.

Now fast-forward to the weekend following my fall colors experience. My daughter hadn't slept well; I was in an argument with my husband; the day turned overcast just as it was time to rake the backyard. I assure you that those glorious leaves didn't inspire me to do anything but grumble, complain, and curse the trees themselves during the long hours it took me to rake them up.

In the last section, we explored being aware of what you take in and on, considering how to set up roadblocks so your exposure to some of the not-so-good stuff out there is limited. Now, we will take a look at the sentiment and attitude that we carry as we approach each day. This is a big one—it's how we show up in the world. It is what we exude and how our energy affects the world around us.

Truth Bomb:

What you notice outside of you is an indication of what is happening inside of you.

Like a mirror, the outside world can often be a reflection of what's happening inside of you. If you are having a bad day, you will be drawn to notice the myriad of reasons to support your sentiment that this day sucks. By the same logic, if you are having a good day, you can find a ton of proof as to why this day is just peachy. We note what is outside of ourselves that matches what we are experiencing on the inside. Consider what you notice the most and think about what that means for your inner landscape.

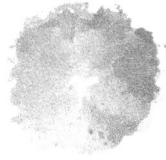

Chapter 7:
EMOTIONAL WEATHER PATTERNS

EACH DAY, AS WE WALK AROUND on planet Earth, we are subject to many different conditions, inputs, and experiences. We are all spinning around through our lives, bouncing off each other and sharing bits and pieces of our attitudes and our energies. The way we show up affects other people, and the way they show up affects us.

POSITIVE FEELINGS

When someone is feeling good, it's easy to see and even easier to be around. There are more smiles, compliments, jokes, and laughter. There's a friendliness and easiness to people when they lead with positive emotions like empathy, confidence, peace, joy, compassion, and love.

Usually, we know when we are feeling good. At those times, we can consciously choose to share that "goodness" with others. So next time you feel yourself flying high on cloud nine, consider doing the following to amplify that goodness:

Drop kindness bombs: As you go through your day, look deeply at the faces of the people around you. These are your fellow humans, traversing the Earth at the same time as you. They are going through their own pain and joy, living and loving just as you are. Try to spread the goodness you're feeling to the other people you come into contact with by dropping kindness bombs. What sort of kindness bomb can you drop on them, either silently or out loud, both to the people you know and to the ones you don't? Maybe you could brighten their day with a simple compliment? Or how about helping them in some way? Maybe hold open the door, pick up something they dropped, or grace them with a genuine smile as they pass by. Niceness doesn't cost you anything, but it can brighten the entire day for the person on the receiving end.

NEGATIVE FEELINGS

The emotions that are perhaps the most detrimental—and sadly, most contagious—are the negative emotions. The good news is that feeling down or upset can provide the necessary contrast to remember how wonderful it is when we feel good. The bad news is that we live in a society that normalizes, and even glorifies, some seriously yucky behaviors like greed and power grabs, materialism, working yourself to death, having little to no exposure to nature. It's no wonder that many of us are running ragged, feeling more despair, jealousy, anger, pain, or sadness than ever before. Fear is generally at the root of a negative emotion, and it can be all encompassing. Good news, though, fellow warriors, much of the fear that you experience is not to be trusted.

There are two distinctly different types of fear. The first is an alert to real danger. Think about walking alone at night and seeing a human-shaped figure lurking in the shadows up ahead. Your body has a physical reaction to that experience, and it puts all of your senses on high alert. That sort of fear causes your body to go into fight-or-flight mode and serves as a protection mechanism to keep you safe. That fear is undeniably helpful and could save your life. It is also experienced far less than the other type of fear: the "what if" fear.

Ahh, fear, my old foe. There have been many flavors of fear in my life. A short, in-no-way-complete list of the many things I am now, or have been in the past, fearful of:

* Doing math in front of other people
* Change
* Loss of a loved one
* Illness
* Pandemics
* Open water
* Car accident
* Flying in anything but the window seat on a plane
* Snakes
* Sharks
* Passing out in public
* Making a buffoon of myself on stage
* Losing my health
* People finding out I don't actually know how to write a book (shh, don't tell anyone!)

Truth Bomb:

"What if" fear is fake.

"What if" fear is an unpleasant emotion caused by an inner concern that a situation could occur that will be embarrassing, threatening, or painful. "What if" fear is imaginary—it is expectation-based worry about a potential future situation. We imagine "what if" situations all the time. "What if I get into a car accident?" "What if he doesn't like me as much as I like him?" "What if I fall stepping on stage?" Even though these potential situations are not guaranteed, and likely won't ever happen, they can still cause *real* anxiety. "What if" fear is a story you tell yourself based on a worst-case scenario occurring. *What if* you told yourself a different story based on the best-case scenario?

I'm sure this list will grow and shift as time goes on. It's daunting to try to keep track of it, and even more daunting to try to manage and control the events in my life, so none of these situations have a chance to happen. It's a good thing I've learned a pretty big up-level along the way—much of the fear I feel is not to be taken seriously and it's *certainly* not to be used as a deterrent to doing or trying something that excites me. Seneca the Younger, a Stoic philosopher in Ancient Rome, said: "We suffer more in imagination than we do in reality." Truth!

Though fear threatens to put me in a chokehold whenever it bursts, Kool-Aid-guy style, through the wall of my mind, I have learned that I can be scared and do the "big things" anyway. Many I have done despite the fear that was with me through it:

* Moving across the country
* Going out in my yard despite the six-foot bull snake I had seen there the day before
* Public speaking for my first few big gigs
* Bodybuilding competition
* Asking someone I admire to be my mentor
* Demanding that my salary be right-sized when I knew it wasn't where it should be
* Birthing other humans—and then being responsible for their care
* Doing math in public

It's been these experiences, and many more, that have, over time, allowed me to build up my confidence. Ralph Waldo Emerson famously said, "Do the thing that you fear and the death of fear is certain." Smart guy.

Despite how yucky fear, stress, and other negative emotions can feel when you are wading through them, in smaller doses, this is all a necessary and regular part of the human experience. Sadness, anxiety, hurt, frustration, and guilt can all be found in healthy human beings. So, if we accept that these negative emotions *will* be there from time to time, then we can roll with it. We don't need to identify with those feelings or allow them to take us over, but we can witness them. We can learn from them. Try to identify the bright side of the negative emotions, such as how anger can also be used as a motivator or frustration can be fuel to figure out a new pathway forward. Don't cower before the negative emotions and don't allow yourself to become swallowed up by them. Observe what's going on and be curious about why it's happening. There is always a lesson for you in times of struggle, so be open to learning what that might be.

It's all too easy today to distract yourself from what you are feeling with your phone, or alcohol, drugs, food, sex, TV, and more. Negative emotions are an indication that there's something you have to work through; there is a truth that is waiting to be uncovered. Get curious about why you are feeling this way and accept the invitation to go deeper inside yourself. You can't run from something within you. You have to turn and face the issue(s). Pema Chödrön writes: "Nothing ever goes away until it teaches us what we need to know."[11] Yes! It's in working through, not around, your issues that you can release them and move forward. This is a golden opportunity to grow.

Truth Bomb:

It's OKAY to throw yourself a time-boxed pity party.

When something happens that takes your emotional train off its usual steady track, it is necessary to give yourself some time to process and allow those emotions to pass through you. Ignoring how you feel and forcefully moving on is a great way for those emotions to get stuck inside of you. Emotions that are bottled up will always come back, usually when your guard is down. So commit to taking time to really feel what you are going through, but do not allow yourself to wallow there. Be courageous enough to dry your tears, tie up your hair, make a cup of something hot, and take another step, even if it's a baby step, on the path toward well-being.

Although I do love looking on the bright side of life, I do not recommend that you bolt on some rose-colored glasses and ignore what you are actually going through. Speaking from experience as your fellow human, until we reach enlightenment, it is simply impossible to be positive and cheerful *all* the time. We are all humans here, and ignoring that sometimes crap just plain stinks would be a dangerous mistake. It's important to be authentic in your experience.

However, you still need to be aware of how you come off to other people. If you are consistently bringing other people down with your negativity, well, quit it! They are all going through their own stuff, too, and likely have more than enough on their plates without you dumping your leftovers on as well.

If you find yourself struggling with negative emotions, there are two helpful practices that can propel you forward into a lighter mood: forgiveness and gratitude.

Forgiveness (for yourself and for others): Holding on to anger or resentment is like taking small doses of poison on a regular basis. Forgiveness is key, but it is not an overnight change. You generally don't just wake up one day and feel A-OK that someone stole your car or that your good friend slept with your boyfriend. It takes time and consideration to be able to look at what has occurred in your life and understand how it has helped you get to where you want to be.

It is critical to remember that you do have a choice in how you feel. This doesn't mean you should push the negative feelings away. It means working through those feelings by witnessing them with the intention of finding the lesson you've learned through that hurt. Acknowledge what happened and take steps to forgive whoever hurt you. This is an extremely difficult exercise in advanced personal development, so be gentle with yourself. It won't be easy.

Remembering that you had to go through that experience to up-level your emotional strength can help.

Perhaps the most important part of the forgiveness lesson is learning to forgive yourself. We are often our own worst critics and can be especially tough on ourselves. Self-forgiveness is an ongoing practice that takes calculated effort, deep work, and heaps of self-love.

When we embrace how flawed we human beings actually are—starting with ourselves—it becomes easier to forgive ourselves and others. None of us are perfect. Making mistakes is a part of our human experience. This is how we learn and grow. Giving ourselves and others space to mess up and still be truly forgiven is the key to moving forward with a clear heart.

Gratitude: Do you ever catch yourself chasing happiness in something new? Future-state desires, such as "if I got this" or "when that happens" are nice for goal setting and proactive planning, but check yourself if these desires become an indication of something you *need* to be happy. A far better use of your brain is to look around and be grateful for where you are right now. Your current reality is likely based on the dreams of your not-so-distant past self. Take the time to be thankful for where you actually are instead of postponing your happiness for a future possibility.

Moreover, being in the habit of noting what you are thankful for can actually change the circuitry of the human brain. Contributor Jennifer Garman quotes the following in a *Thrive Global* article written in 2020: "According to the UCLA Mindfulness Awareness Research Center, 'regularly expressing gratitude (the quality of being thankful and the readiness to show appreciation) literally changes the molecular structure of the brain, keeps the gray matter functioning, and makes us healthier and happier.'"[12]

I tend to weave in and out of a dedicated gratitude practice. When negative feelings take hold of me for longer than I'm comfortable with, I know it's time to prioritize a more steady gratitude practice again. Stating what I am grateful for helps me reconnect to the already-present contentment and peace in my life.

There are many different ways to start your own gratitude practice. Some people like to carry a small, dedicated-to-gratitude notebook around with them to capture an ongoing list of everything they are grateful for. Some people start their day with gratitude, taking a moment to be thankful that they woke up warm and safe in their beds. Others close out the day with a mental list of the favorable events that happened throughout their day. Develop the practice that works best for you to stay connected to everything you are thankful for.

A NOTE ABOUT CHRONIC STRESS

Intentionally being able to overcome negative feelings is a great way to maintain ongoing, long-term mental health. It is awesome if you are able to do that on your own. Add that to your gratitude list! However, if you are one of the millions of people who find themselves unable to feel better no matter what they've tried, I beseech you to waste no time in seeking out a professional who can help.

The long-term effects of stress on the human mind and body are not for the faint of heart, literally. Over time, chronic stress can cause serious heart disease, like high blood pressure, heart attack, and stroke. Mentally, chronic stress can lead to depression and anxiety. We carry a terrible stigma in the United States around mental health that needs to be changed. We have all climbed a different ladder of life experiences that have led to this moment in time. No one of us is in a place to judge another. Many of the most successful people I know are also the first ones to ask for help when they need it.

If you are struggling, seek out the resources that can help. I preemptively commend you for taking whatever steps are needed to get yourself into a place of optimal mental health.

MIXED FEELINGS

Human emotions are often far more complex than this or that, happy or sad, good or bad. Most of what I feel is a mixture of different emotions.

For example, bittersweet is a common feeling I have as a parent. I am thankful for the lovely, innocent joy I see on my children's faces, but at the same time, I can feel sad or anxious about what I know life will hurl at them.

When an elderly or sick family member or friend finally passes away after a long and painful illness, it can incite mixed emotions, especially of grief and relief. Grief at the loss you've experienced alongside relief that your loved one is no longer suffering.

Feeling scared and excited has always been an important emotional blend for me. It usually accompanies a stretch project or big goal that I've committed to undertake. Those emotions are an indication that I'm doing something significant on my life path. When I began speaking at large conferences, I was simultaneously crippled by fear and propelled by excitement to do my best.

If you ever feel this particular blend of mixed emotions, I *implore* you to say yes to the thing that is making you feel that way. It means that when you have completed whatever the mission is, you will be granted a hyper-dose of personal growth. Level up, here you come!

As you consider the descriptions and examples of positive, negative, and mixed feelings presented in this chapter, here are some questions to ask yourself about your emotional landscape:

* Do you usually approach your day with positivity and enthusiasm, looking for the bright side of life? Or do you tend to focus on the negative or lack in situations?

* Do you practice kindness? Do you inspire or encourage the people around you? Do you champion their successes? Or are you resentful and judgy?

* Are you grateful for the multitude of blessings you have in your world? Or do you find yourself focused on a sense of lack in your life?

* Do you allow emotions to run their course naturally? Or do you try to push away what you consider to be "bad"?

* Do you look for the lessons in your life? Or do you tend to shy away from looking too deeply at what you've experienced?

TRY THIS

A challenge: Try to listen to your mind chatter during the next stressful situation that comes along. How can you reframe your thoughts to highlight gratitude instead of negativity and lack? Here are some examples:

* "Ugh. I feel so frazzled after this crazy day at work."
  * Reframe: I am healthy inside, and I have a job that challenges me.

* "This house is a mess, and my guests are almost here!"
  * Reframe: I have a home, I have friends. We can all be safe inside, warm and together.
* "I sooo don't want to go grocery shopping."
  * Reframe: I have enough money to buy the food that I need, and it's all available at a store right down the street.

WHY

Every interaction that we have with the people around us affects them too. Becoming more conscious of how you approach your day-to-day will allow you to, powerfully and positively, shift your attitude. Mahatma Gandhi said, "You must be the change you wish to see in the world." Give out what you want to receive back. Forget about perfection and instead strive for progress. Own all your feelings without fully identifying with them by keeping in mind that they are transient—yours as well as the feelings of others. Don't take negative things that happen outside of you personally. Lean in to the positive and model what a brightly shining person looks like. You will inspire others to do the same.

If you approach each new day—for the most part, because we are all human here—with a big dose of compassion, love, and joy, those feelings will rub off on the other people you encounter. Each positive interaction that we have provides a double dose of goodness, one for you and one for whoever else gets to feel your good vibes. Be the first wave of kindness and goodness that will ripple through the next person along the way.

Chapter 8:
STOP RUSHING

I'M EMBARRASSED TO ADMIT that I spent about four years rushing through my life. I mean, taking almost zero time to smell the roses. I was busy accomplishing thing after thing, trying to shave seconds off each task during the day, in a feeble attempt to gain a minute or two back at the end of the day for . . . I don't know what.

I do have to give that younger me credit for making it through, though, because those were tough years. I was a very young single mother, living far away from my core family. Survival was the name of the game, and I suppose rushing helped me get through the responsibilities of each day as quickly as possible. But the sad reality is that in the constant whirlwind of running from one thing to the next, my head was completely out of sync with what my body was doing. I was thinking mostly of the future, or sometimes the past, but never the *now*.

THE CYCLE OF BUSY

Let's see if this sounds familiar to you:

Alarm. Wake up, check email. Stumble out of bed. Quick shower, think about the pending chaos of the day to come. Get ready, get the kid up, make breakfast. Bolt from the house like a bat out of hell. Rush the kid to school. Rush yourself to work. Whirlwind day of meetings and calls and rushing, including rushed apologies for having to take a potty break on your way to the tenth meeting of the day. Scram out of work to go pick up the kid. Get home. Throw dinner together. Homework, bath, story, bedtime. Wine. Collapse on the couch. Fall asleep checking social media. Wake up. Rinse and repeat.

This was how I functioned in the past, and I *know* this is not just my story. In fact, this is a common narrative I hear from my friends, coworkers, and family members. Ask people how they are and get the usual: "Things are great, just suuuuuper busy." Are we all actually that busy? Why such *rush*?

OUR SOCIETY IS SET UP FOR BUSY

Our society is set up to feed us more and more and more. We are pinged constantly by IMs, phone calls, emails, social media notifications, and text messages. This diminishes our attention span to almost nothing, and we jump without purpose from one thing to the next without really being where we are.

In addition to having to manage so much additional stimuli, we also use the "Busy Badge of Honor" in conversations with friends and family. "Busy" has become a totally bonkers status symbol that we throw around at each other like some weird game of catch. Are we bragging? Are we complaining? Why is "busy" such a go-to answer when asked how we are?

In a fascinating study called "Conspicuous Consumption of Time: When Busyness and Lack of Leisure Time Become a Status Symbol"[13] researcher Silvia Bellezza, a professor of marketing at Columbia Business School, set up an experiment to gauge how a specific type of social media posts would affect the reader's assumptions about that person. Bellezza presented study participants with two types of social media profiles: one with status updates that stress a consistent busyness at work, and another with status updates that reflect a more leisurely lifestyle. The goal was to find out what the participants would assume about these people. The results were abundantly clear that in the US, people think that the busier a person is, the higher their status must be. Makes me think of that poor fly that spends exhausting hours banging into the same spot on the window. Yeah, that guy is definitely busy, but dropping dead of exhaustion—while still *inside*—doesn't seem like it qualifies as a high-status activity to me. In my years of rush, I felt like that fly, exhausted and getting nowhere.

MY TURNING POINT

One day, on my rush home from work, so I could begin rushing through my evening at home, I was pulled over. I had been driving dangerously fast in a residential zone. The police officer who stood outside my car asked a plain question: "Why are you speeding?" I opened my mouth to answer him, but nothing came out. I had nothing. There was no excuse for me going so fast. The truth is that I was on autopilot, with my one speed set to GO NOW. I suppose my frazzled and lost look inspired the cop to let me go with a warning, and I drove off with his words ringing in my head: SLOW DOWN!

This small interaction took maybe ten minutes of my time, but it planted within me a seed of "maybe I *don't* have to rush so much?" I got home ten minutes later than usual that day, and lo and behold, the world continued to turn.

I began to see subtle signs and indications that encouraged me to stop rushing. Those signs may not be as clear as a police officer standing beside your car, but when our minds are open to seeing them, they can be just as powerful. For me, this showed up as a general sense of feeling incomplete and unfulfilled. I felt an itching jealousy when other people shared their good news. I felt a constant, low-grade worry that I was missing out on my son's youth. These thoughts, and so many others, were impossible to fully feel or understand when my head was so disconnected from my body. But when I slowed down for even a few seconds, I was better able to notice what my quiet inner voice was saying, and the message was clear: It's time for a change.

HOW TO STOP

Over time, and with some heavy-duty soul-searching, I came to the realization that there are only so many hours in the day, and all my rushing around could never change that. But what I could do is create more depth within the time I do have by reattaching my head to my body and fully experiencing the present moment. I developed a routine of a few simple steps to follow each time I felt myself getting sucked in by the rush. This was a game changer for me. Next time you catch yourself rushing, I dare you to try it.

1. Take a breath. Countdown from 5-4-3-2-1 and take long, rejuvenating, conscious breaths as you go.
2. Notice what's happening around you. Experience this moment through the senses you were gifted with: look, listen, smell, taste, feel.
3. Don't resist the present moment by thinking about the future or the past. Focus on whatever you are doing at this moment, and enjoy the beautiful simplicity of the NOW.

Bonus points if you are able to attach some gratitude to this practice. Let's say you are stuck in traffic and anxiously trying to get somewhere. Instead of leaning forward and tap-tap-tapping the wheel, sit back and breathe. Be thankful that you are alive and of sound mind and body to drive, that you have a working car and places to go. Try to be mindful, and thankful, for exactly where you are.

BENEFITS OF SLOWING DOWN

I would like to say that I never rush around anymore; however, that's just not true. I do. But I'm better able to spot when it's happening and, therefore, better able to shift gears. When things begin to blur for me, I have conditioned myself to remember that there is no point in looking for extra minutes in the day because they don't exist. But I can expand the minutes I do have by shifting my mindset, breathing into the present moment, and fully experiencing what I'm doing.

Truth Bomb:

Your power is in the present.

The present moment is where your power is. It's not in reliving past situations; it's not in worrying about what will or won't happen in the future. It's today, in this moment, in the now. As you sit in your home, with your family or friends or pets or with yourself. You are alive; you have enough food to eat and all the clean water you can drink. Fresh air to breathe and the mental and physical capacity to do anything you want. Look around, take stock, be grateful. As the late, but oh-so-great, Ram Dass so succinctly wrote and taught: "Be here now."[14]

If having more depth, more peace, and deeper experiences sounds good to you (and if you are reading this, I bet it does), *stop rushing*. Please consider this your official permission to *s l o w d o w n*. To spend more time with yourself or those around you in the present moment. It's more peaceful in the present when you can shed the regrets of yesterday and the shoulds of tomorrow. The bounty of awesome is right here, right now. What a concept that is! A world of wonder, patiently lying in wait for whenever you are ready to slow down enough to experience it.

TRY THIS

Here are some ways to slow down and flex into your present power:

* Use your senses to be fully in the moment. Enjoy the taste and the smell of the food you are eating. Eat it slowly, mindfully. Note the temperature of the water you are drinking. Feel the softness of a summer breeze on your skin. Note the vibrant color of the flower you are gazing at. Really feel your child's hand in yours. Let music pulse through your body and listen deeply, feel it.

* When you are in conversation with someone, give them the gift of your full presence and attention. Make sure you are truly there for them, deeply listening, not just waiting to talk.

* When you find yourself slipping into the past to replay an old situation or future tripping about something that hasn't happened yet, gently bring yourself back into the present by stating what those thoughts represent: *memory* for past reenactments and *imagination* for future ideations.

WHY

At the highest level, the beneficial act of slowing down will increase presence. Presence is rewarded with awareness. Awareness turns up the volume and clarity on everyday, ordinary moments because you can experience them with all of your senses. Experiences will begin to feel new. You will be able to connect with others on a deeper level and build more meaningful relationships when you are able to truly hear and see them. You can better immerse yourself in your work or your passions and experience a sense of flow, where you delightfully lose yourself in the activity, and time seems to stand still. You will notice the little things and get more enjoyment from the simple pleasures that are easy to overlook when your mind is constantly jumping around to the past or the future.

Awareness also helps you make better sense of your inner experiences and develop a deeper understanding of yourself. And that is precisely what we are here to do. So stop rushing and open the door to a myriad of changes—for the *way better*, that are already within your reach.

Chapter 9:
START HELPING

SOCIAL PSYCHOLOGIST ELIZABETH DUNN has spent years studying the science of happiness and positivity. She advises this: "Let's stop thinking about giving as just this moral obligation and start thinking of it as a source of pleasure."[15] I love this concept!

I'm sure there are a myriad of science-rooted reasons why this is the case, likely having to do with the fact that we are a social species, and helping one another has been key to our collective survival. But you don't have to be a scientist to understand that there is a great value in taking the focus off of your obsessions.

We spend so much time living locked up inside our minds in an isolated and often destructive way. As social media continues to wrap its white-knuckled grip around our frontal lobes, toxic individualism has become a real thing that we grapple with, mostly at an unconscious level. Toxic individualism is the belief that you are alone in what you are going through, and it couldn't be farther from reality. Thinking "This only happens to me," or "No one will *ever* understand my experience," are indications that you are grappling with toxic individualism. We are all humans, exposed more or less to the same high-level conditions at the same time. There are plenty of other people who can certainly feel our lived experiences to some degree, so those feelings of aloneness are not only unhealthy but also not true. By getting stuck in toxic individualism, we prevent ourselves from seeing our connection to one another, which gives us little opportunity to show kindness toward others and also fosters the ideas of competition and rivalry.

Let me start with a deep *siiiiiiiiiiiiiiigh*. It saddens me that we still need to talk about this, but alas, here we go. There is no reason today that you should feel threatened by the woman next to you. Historically, competition among women has been understandable because we've been treated as a second-class gender. We've had to fight hard to take our place as active members in society with rights and a say in what happens. Since there weren't enough spots at the literal or proverbial table, it made us competitive among ourselves. However, those times are over.

If you see one token woman on the management team at your company today, do you think she is sitting in your spot? Does another woman's beauty somehow diminish yours? Is that woman's relationship with her partner or child somehow related to you in any way? The answers are a resounding no, no, and no. Though gender equality is still painfully unbalanced in leadership in most industries, we can help fix this by lifting one another up.

Truth Bomb:

Other women are not your rivals.

Rivalries among women are a bona fide waste of time. Now, don't get me wrong, you can't be great buds with everyone. But you don't need to perceive other women as a threat to your success or worth. Let that queen stand beside you and shine in her crown. You can still stand proudly alongside her and shine in yours.

In today's world of always-on social media, it's easy, especially when you are feeling low, to tumble down a rabbit hole of comparison with all the "perfect" lives of other women in your feed. Reality check: their lives are *not* perfect. Although it may appear that they have their shit together, chances are, they are grappling with the same messy issues you are.

You are truly in your power when you take responsibility for your actions, emotions, and energies. From that perspective, the only person to strive to be better than is the woman you were yesterday.

Let me tell you about an embroidered piece of artwork that we had hanging up in my childhood home. It featured the word TALK written vertically, and then next to each letter were the words: Try **A** **L**ittle **K**indness. It was framed and displayed in a prominent, highly visible place.

As I grew up, this was "just" another piece of art that hung around the house. I didn't give it much thought. Being kind wasn't in the forefront of my brain while living in a house full of kids and preteens. Racing from door to door to lock my two younger brothers out of the house was far more important, as was listening in on my older sister's phone calls from the landline in the other room or fighting for time on dial-up AOL. These were higher priorities for me than being kind.

Now, as a full-fledged grown-up, watching the people of this crazy world fight and rage and flail around in their territorial outbursts, I think of that sign and am fairly certain it holds the key to resolving some, if not most, of the chaos and unrest we currently see. Even a little kindness can go far. Looks like it's time to dust off the old Golden Rule, eh? It's not only for the people on the receiving end of the kindness either. Kindness has this amazing backward splash effect that benefits the people on the giving end as well.

WAYS TO HELP

As a social species, humans are hardwired for community. Performing acts of service helps create those human-to-human bonds by connecting us on a deeper level with those we may never have had the chance to meet otherwise. Here are some ways you can sprinkle some of the good, serviced-based pleasure on yourself by helping others:

Monetary Donations: This is a hands-free financial donation, either as a one-off or on a regular basis. Giving money where and when it's needed, as in for a specific geographical area that has been affected by a natural disaster or toward a medical research organization, offers support to many. You are giving toward a cause rather than to a specific person.

Service and Volunteering: This is one of the strongest ways you can feel the kickback of helping because it allows you to witness the goodness of your supportive actions through direct contact with the recipient. Volunteering at a soup kitchen, being involved with a refugee program, being connected with a child through the Big Brothers Big Sisters of America program, or delivering meals to a senior center are all examples of getting directly involved.

Truth Bomb:

There is a psychological benefit when you help other people.

Ironically enough, serving other people is a critical part of self-care, as the act of service provides surprisingly positive benefits for the person performing the "selfless" action. Helping other people creates the connections that we so sorely need in our divided world. Kindness is the inspiration to act, helping is the action, and connection is the reward. Try to find a way to help at least one person every day and see how you feel.

Coming face-to-face with the person you are serving has been shown to be the most rewarding type of giving. There are a variety of options for extending this type of help. Get to Google and start searching for a reputable organization near you. Then, see how you feel after you volunteer.

Small Acts of Kindness: This is by far my favorite option, as it doesn't take any fore-planning or time commitment. Random acts of kindness happen organically throughout the day and need no prompting, no rules. The only requirement is that you allow your heart to lead the way during any given interaction with another person. This can be as simple as holding open a door for the human coming in behind you. Or tapping your brakes so someone else can get in front of you instead of speeding up so they can't. Or offering a genuine smile to a stranger or a helping hand to someone who is struggling to carry their packages.

How about challenging yourself to pay a stranger an honest compliment once a day? Try it and see how you feel. I've done this, and I have to say, the compliment has a sweet bounce-back effect. It takes you just a couple of seconds to do this, but it could change the tone of that person's entire day, and yours.

There are so many negative interactions that take place between people. Why not see what happens when we drop some coins into the bank of positive interactions?

Mentorship: Mentorship is far more of a time-and-energy commitment, but it's so powerful. The benefits for both parties can be life changing.

Climbing, in your career and life, and carrying someone else along with you is the way to go. In my particular situation, mentorship has been an integral piece of my career path. I have been extremely fortunate to have had some extraordinary mentors throughout my career and am now carrying that forward with mentees of my own.

I believe we can all benefit from a mentor, no matter our career or success level. Mentorship doesn't have to flow in any particular direction or be tied to age. There are always multiple generations sharing space in the workforce, so we have ample opportunity to learn from different people with different experiences. If you can open yourself to see mentorship with a 360-degree view, you will have more options for what mentorship might look like in your life.

TRY THIS

Look back at the list of ways to help other people. Which of these can you commit to doing today? If none of them sound feasible to you, why is that? When we are too caught up in our own minds, it can be extremely difficult to see things outside of ourselves with clarity. Try refocusing your attention on how you might offer small, intentional acts of kindness that treat other people with compassion, respect, and understanding. Even if it's as simple as a genuine compliment, note how you feel when you witness someone take in your kind gesture or words. The power of that act can help you both feel better.

WHY

It's time that we all start actively looking for opportunities to help other people. To do our part to live up to the *kind* in humankind. We are all fumbling around, trying to figure out this world. By being kinder to one another through simple but powerful acts of goodness, we can help create a more compassionate and harmonious world. I would love to see what our society might look like with kindness as a large-scale, main driver of human behavior. Maybe that sign hanging on my parents' wall is *the* sign that we all need to be reminded of? Try a little kindness. It's worth it.

LIFE LESSON 4:

Treat Yourself Lovingly

**"I have come to believe that caring
for myself is not self-indulgent Caring
for myself is an act of survival."** [16]

—Audre Lorde, American writer, womanist, radical
feminist, professor, and civil rights activist

OH BOY, OH JOY—HIGH FIVE up top because it is now time to shift our focus to a crucially important practice for anyone who wants to be truly, and sustainably, successful: treating yourself with care, kindness, love, and compassion.

We all know that life can be really tough, with a dizzying variety of personal and professional issues hurled at us every day. We do our best to balance all the fastballs, curveballs, and screwballs, but there will always be the next uncomfortable situation lurking around the corner that we have to deal with.

So, how do you withstand all the outside pressures? You take care of the *inside* through a regular practice of radical self-care.

Self-care has long been synonymous with bubble baths and the beautiful yet weary woman taking a peaceful moment for herself. This is important, yes—and *man,* do I love a super-hot-to-the-point-of-boiling bubble bath. However, it's nowhere near enough to encompass what actually needs to happen to treat yourself lovingly. Treating yourself lovingly involves practicing self-compassion, nurturing yourself, and prioritizing your holistic well-being. At the highest level, these are the building blocks of radical self-care.

Truth Bomb:

The term "self-care" is long overdue for redefinition.

Historically, self-care is a drastically misunderstood concept with a narrow definition. Real, radical self-care goes far beyond just isolated, time-boxed activities like getting a massage or going on a retreat. For it to be truly and deeply effective, it should encompass aspects and activities from the perspective of physical, mental, emotional, and spiritual health. Radical self-care must be practiced with daily life regularity. It is never selfish. It is a critical practice to maintain long-term health and well-being, which helps you to show up in a more positive and balanced way for those around you.

Radical self-care encompasses behaviors like attending a long girls' weekend with your besties or taking a new class. It also applies to smaller actions, like drinking more water or taking a nap when your body wants one. It's about being mindful and present, setting boundaries, and learning how to soothe yourself when things get rough. It's about resting when you need to, reflecting, and curbing bad habits and creating good ones. It's as big as a long-dreamed-about cross-country move and as small as allowing yourself that one moment when you are doing laundry and that fresh-from-the-dryer, good-smelling, warm blanket comes out, and you wrap it around yourself, giving you a momentary, delicious *pause*.

Think you don't have time for any of that? Right, I know. None of us do. But consider it like this: how many people rely on you to show up for them? Who benefits from you martyring yourself and burning out? If you are guilty of burning the candle at both ends—and we all are from time to time—then this is your call to action to sprinkle in more self-care throughout your day. You have to charge your own battery if you expect to keep using your power bank to give others a boost.

Unless you won the super-woke-person-close-to-you-at-a-critical-age lottery, chances are good that you were never taught much about self-love. Although it bubbles up from time to time in recent history (thank you, Mr. Rogers, Louise Hay, Maya Angelou, Jesus, and a growing number of other excellent examples of human beings), it hasn't been much of a part of our regular daily conversation. School is great at teaching you math, reading, and social skills. Society teaches you to fit in and consume and work to have the prescribed life. Traditional religion touches on self-love, but it's often coupled with serious guilt or other lengthy rules and conditions and, therefore, takes the wind out of the "treating your-self lovingly" sails.

Truly caring for yourself, inside and out, is something that needs to be considered, practiced, and honored on a daily basis. Good news here, though: this is the *best* stuff. Treating yourself like a long-lost best friend, figuring out how to heal yourself, and prioritizing what you love the most? Pssssh. Where do I sign?

Chapter 10:
TREAT YOURSELF PHYSICALLY

A FEW YEARS BACK, I decided to enter a fitness competition. You know the ones: sparkly bikinis, spray tans, clear heels, muscles galore. Almost like a strip show but with more pausing, posing, and the tiny triangles of insanely expensive material required to stay on. Yup. This was what I decided I wanted to do with my free time.

Arriving at the decision to do this happened in the most benign and random way. I had been working out at the gym when a stranger came by and asked me what I was training for. I didn't understand the question at first. Training for . . . what, exactly? Was there a right answer beyond "to look and feel good" or "because this is what I've always done?" After thinking about it for some time, I thought, "Well, shit, maybe I should be training *for* something." I had seen those fitness show competitions and had always wondered what went into them. I do love a huge goal, so I decided to make it happen.

For the next twelve weeks, I worked my butt off—literally. I hired a fitness coach, adopted a rigorous diet and workout schedule, and subjected myself to regular size-ups and weigh-ins, complete with routine prodding and pinching to test my body fat. I spent more time analyzing every inch of my body in front of the mirror than I had ever done before.

When it was all said and done, I was in the best shape of my life. Tight, fit, and toned. But emotionally, I had never felt worse.

As it turns out, although I had always kept some degree of focus on my personal fitness, when I entered the competition, my perspective of myself drastically changed. When I agreed to be judged by someone else's set of criteria, all the fun was stripped away from my workouts and an unprecedented level of insecurity crept in. I was incredibly critical of every inch of my body. As a result, I spent a lot more time hiding in baggy T-shirts and sweatpants so I wouldn't have to see my body.

As a goal-driven person, once I sign up for something, I'm damn well finishing it, so I followed through. On the day of the competition, I plastered on a fake tan and fake smile. I spun and twirled and flexed. And I didn't place.

It wasn't much of a surprise that I didn't do very well. No awards or trophies were bestowed upon me that day. I gave myself credit for doing the big, new thing I had set out to do, but the only real win that day was learning something new about myself. I don't think I had even left the competition venue before I vowed that competition would be my one and only. It just wasn't right for me. I met a lot of great people along the way, most of whom loved the experience and went on to do more competitions, but for me, this was the end. Preparing for that competition had taken me farther away from loving my physical body than when I started. Not at all my style.

SAY THANK YOU TO THE BODY

It would be a mistake to ignore that we all have complicated relationships with our bodies. I'm sure we all have body parts that we wish were different. Many of us (me included) have taken steps to remove, change, or enhance some part we didn't like in its original form. People with chronic illness, disease, or other physical ailments could certainly give you their hit list of what they would trade or replace. Despite all that, there is still an intentional thank you that we owe these bodies, no matter how flawed they may sometimes seem.

Here are a few reasons why this wonderful Earth Suit deserves your express thanks, pronto:

It's automatic: What a wonderful operating system your body has! It breathes by itself; it digests your food; it keeps all internal systems going auto-magically. And it moves! You just think about moving, and then, wow! Off it goes, literally allowing you to get after anything you want to experience more of. I understand that it can become difficult to hold gratitude for your Earth Suit when you are unable to move all parts or to move without experiencing pain. How might you be able to acknowledge what it does provide?

It's resilient: The body is incredibly adaptable. It can heal itself (what a feature that is!), working hard to squash bugs and viruses on autopilot. You can push it to the max physically, and it will respond, adapt, and become stronger. And it can bounce back after you try to poison it with too much of the wrong food, alcohol, or drugs. Amazing!

Truth Bomb:

Be super grateful for your super Earth Suit.

Honesty check: Do you take it for granted when your body is working properly? I sure do. It's far easier to spot when something is painful or not working right. What if we could get into the practice of noting the physical parts we are thankful for instead of fixating on what we don't like? These Earth Suits do so much for us every day. Get into the practice of dropping regular, intentional, and heartfelt thank yous to your perfectly imperfect body for the way it carries you through life.

It comes with senses: Holy moly, your body comes pre-built with some incredibly enhanced features. You can taste, smell, touch, hear, see, and feel. Through the body, you can truly experience the richness of the world around you, which helps you land right in the present moment, whenever you choose to.

It's uniquely yours: The Earth Suit you are driving was designed 100 percent just for you. It is a fully custom model, one-of-a-kind, limited edition. It's perfectly suited to express your emotions, hug your loved ones, and explore the passions and projects you want.

So, despite its flaws, I suggest you get on board right now with being thankful for this amazing gift. Just because it's always been there with you doesn't mean you can't think about it now with a renewed sense of childlike wonder. Cultivating deep gratitude for this Earth Suit will literally make you feel more at home in your own skin.

PUT THE GOOD STUFF IN THE TANK

One of the coolest features about these Earth Suits is that they are perfectly designed to benefit from the stuff that grows on the Earth. Imagine that! It's like we are meant to be here. Reward yourself with natural, healthy, unprocessed foods that give you energy and make you feel great. Drink lots and lots of water. Get big doses of clean air and sunshine.

And certainly don't neglect exercise. Exercise is a cornerstone practice for keeping the body feeling and looking good. There are so many different ways to do this that you can definitely find whatever works best for you. We needn't all be gym rats. The Earth is a veritable playground of different places to explore and ways to move, so get creative. Try taking a walk, a hike, a swim, a run. Skate around, hop on a bike, climb up something, jump over something, or dance and twirl around your kitchen—or better yet, around your neighborhood like a happy fool. Find a movement-based activity that you enjoy and then do it again and again.

PRIORITIZE REST AND RELAXATION

In today's world, we are able to work almost nonstop, we forfeit our earned vacation time, and we wear the word "busy" as a badge of honor. No wonder that taking time for some real-deal, high-quality R&R is one of those areas that we struggle with the most. When life has you in its "go-go-go" grip, the thought, or even worse—the practice, of carving out time to rest is almost unimaginable. Or if you have young kids, this might be something that you try to do, but in reality, it is interrupted with astonishing regularity. Either way, prioritizing rest and downtime in your life, and actually making it happen, is a game changer. Burnout is bogus. Taking time to recharge is a critical, healthy, nonnegotiable part of being a whole person.

TRY THIS

Take a moment to think of everything you love about your body. What does your body do for you? How do you feel when you truly consider that this body is the best, most advanced vehicle you will ever drive?

Then, from that frame of mind, honestly answer the following questions:

Question 1: Are you feeling less-than-fine about anything you regularly put into your body?

Meat and alcohol have recently come up on this list for me. To be honest, I'm not ready to remove either completely, but being aware of how I feel when I eat meat or drink alcohol has paved the way for me to take steps to limit my intake of both, and I already feel better for it.

Question 2: What can you add to your repertoire that would make you feel better physically?

More movement? More water? Vegetables? Vitamins? I'm betting there's something that arises here for you. Why not test it out and give it a try? Then, see how you feel, and if you like how you're feeling, add more.

Question 3: With a new acknowledgment that your body is a one-of-a-kind, top-shelf, fully customized model made just for you, how does that change the foundation of your relationship with it?

WHY

Whether discontinuing what doesn't feel good or adding what does, your body is well worth the investment of time, attention, and intention. Feeling comfortable in your own body is like having the best accessory that goes with everything. No matter where you are or what you are doing, it feels better to wear the Earth Suit that you feel good about and that you've put time and work into. Feeling good on the inside projects radiance on the outside and shows other people what it can look like when you are comfortable in your own skin.

So take care of that beautiful body of yours! Don't take one day that you are healthy and ambulatory for granted. No matter what your personal gripes or issues with your body, I guarantee you can find thousands of other people who would love to upgrade to your model.

Chapter 11:
TREAT YOURSELF MENTALLY

OH MAN, THESE MINDS OF OURS. They are certainly the most powerful planning, analyzing, and processing tool we have at our disposal. An innate supercomputer that is constantly on, scanning the world around us at light speed, making assessments, judgments, and calling the shots. The mind's main agenda is to keep you safe. The best way to keep you safe is to make sure you stay rooted in the known.

I get it. I have a couple of kiddos kicking around, and the best way for me to keep them safe is to know the environment, reduce the unknowns, and maintain the routine. Safer to watch TV at home than to swim in the ocean. Safer to play a board game than to take a trip to Europe. Unfortunately, this can be boring, unstimulating, and does not foster growth.

Holistic self-care is two-fold: it's about both physical doing and mental being. In this chapter, we are going to look at some great ways to increase your ability to be in a healthy mental state. It begins with an understanding of how your brain operates and then giving said brain a well-deserved break and dose of happiness.

BE YOUR OWN BEST FRIEND

Have you ever really listened to your own inner critic? Or taken the time to consider objectively the nonstop commentary you have running in your mind? In his amazing, bestselling book, *The Untethered Soul: The Journey Beyond Yourself,*[17] Michael Singer likens your inner critic to that of a crazy person who gets to advise you directly 100 percent of the time. Here are some examples:

You: "Oooh, party invite!"
Inner Critic: "Ugh, there will be so many strangers there."

You: "I would love to follow my passion and start a bake shop."
Inner Critic: "Perfect way to waste a ton of time and money. Three-quarters of all new businesses fail in the first year. And what about health insurance?!"

You: "He's super cute. I wonder if I should talk to him?"
Inner Critic: "He probably has a beautiful wife and family."

What if you had a friend who gave you advice like this? How long would that "friend" stay at the top of your text list? Not long. Why then, do we allow that inner critic to advise us every day, all day long?

Becoming aware of this inner critic is the first step toward disidentifying with it. When you catch that voice giving you its patented negative advice, first make note that it's happening, calling it by name. For example, "Negative Nancy is striking again." Then (if you'll allow me to oversimplify a complicated concept), just choose not to listen to it. This is far easier said than done, but having the intention to ignore that negative head trash is the only way you can ever start doing it. Stopping the voice altogether is an incredible feat, though some enlightened beings are able to achieve it. For the average peeps like you and me, though, it's far "easier" to just not listen to the advice.

One technique to help you decouple from your mental madness is to drop your awareness from your head into your heart and try to operate from there. The heart will be better able to remind you of the good that could come in any given situation, without the pressure of trying to keep you safe. Going to the party means you will meet new people. Starting the bake shop means you will have a new life experience. Talking to that man means your emotions might get the opportunity to run wild, and despite where they may end up, it will be worth it. The heart knows far better than the head, and its advice should get top priority.

Another big issue with that inner critic is that it talks shit about you. If you catch yourself being unproductively critical or demeaning toward yourself, that is a bright red flag that should be addressed. Back to the analogy of the friend. Would you keep a friend around who spewed negativity and disdain directly at you? Would you hold her advice in high regard? Hell no, you wouldn't!

Truth Bomb:

Be gentle with yourself.

Life outside of yourself is tough enough without allowing your inside to be tough too. Stressful situations are even more challenging when you are unproductively critical of yourself. Being gentle with ourselves is an essential part of maintaining our overall well-being. When we are comfortable showing ourselves a healthy amount of kindness, we are much more likely to extend kindness to others. It's not always easy to be gentle with ourselves, and it shouldn't be confused with self-indulgence or self-pity. Instead, it is about treating ourselves with the same compassion, care, and understanding we would offer to a good friend.

Here is some guidance to keep in mind as you, *finally*, become your own best friend:

1. **Give yourself a break.** Life is tough, and you are doing an admirable job of figuring out some really serious stuff. Stop with the shoulds and the trash talk. You are good enough as you were, as you are, and as you will be.
2. **Celebrate your wins.** Note and honor when you have completed something that was difficult. Take yourself out, raise a glass to yourself, or at the very least, make a mental note of your accomplishment.
3. **Forgive yourself and others.** We humans make mistakes, which is always okay as long as we learn from them. Apologize when needed, including to yourself, and move on.
4. **Trust yourself.** Learn to do the gut check, and then (super important) heed the gut's advice. When considering a decision, get quiet and explore how the various options would make you feel. You'll know what you should do by how you feel inside. A decision that is aligned with your gut will evoke feelings of calm. A decision that is misaligned will evoke feelings of agitation. Your instincts will never steer you wrong.

BE PLAYFUL

Most of the women I meet through Healthy Women Leaders don't have much trouble with their work ethic. So many of them are making amazing strides in life, driving their careers and families forward at an impressive pace. But if that's all you do, then I have a news alert for you: It's time to make some room for play in your life.

Working yourself to the point of burnout is so last decade. It's not sustainable and, quite honestly, it's not a good look on you. To be truly healthy, you have to figure out how to balance all that great work with a big dose of fun. What is an activity or a passion you have that makes you laugh, feel stimulated, silly, or free? What do you do that gives you the warm and fuzzy feels? Find that thing and commit to prioritizing it and incorporating it into your world. Life doesn't have to be so serious! Relax a bit and allow yourself to float on a current of fun and lightheartedness.

BE CREATIVE

For many of us, creativity has become a relic of childhood. It's something we *used* to do. We played make-believe; we drew with crayons; we made creatures with Play-Doh. We got messy, imagined shapes in the clouds, and ran amok, soaring with our arms outstretched.

And then it stopped. I don't remember when it stopped or why, but it happened to me. Painting was replaced with meeting agendas and proposals. Daydreams gave way to home repairs and bills and babies crying in the night. So how can we get it back?

The first step is to truly miss it, taking yourself back to the times and places when you experienced how great it felt to let your mind run wild. Then, it's time to take adult-sized baby steps back toward that place of creativity within yourself. Make it easy for you to create, with a new journal right where and when you are most likely to write or a sketchbook at your desk for idle hands as you listen to your zillionth Zoom call of the day. How about making up a new dance as you do your hair? And then challenging a family member to do it with you? Introducing small bits of creativity back into your world will open the door for more to follow. Try one small creative activity today—and bonus points if it's the same flavor of creativity you used to love as a kid—and see how it makes you feel.

BE IN NATURE

The way we live today makes it so easy to stay inside and work, watch TV, or stare at our phones constantly. We could literally spend all our waking hours indoors, sitting down, wholly caught up in our minds. This certainly does not sound like fun, and additionally, it's a risk to your health. A sedentary, unbalanced, indoor life can push you quickly toward a myriad of health problems. If we don't intentionally strive for a more balanced existence, we will never find one. The good news: The most perfectly beautiful, vastly diverse, and vibrantly alive planet is waiting right outside of our doors.

As we slip farther and farther away from the natural elements, it's no shock that in recent years, doctors and psychologists have begun to prescribe that people get outside as a form of therapy. **Grounding** (walking with your bare feet on the earth), **forest bathing** (spending quiet time in a forest atmosphere, taking in the present moment with all of your senses), and generally **connecting yourself closer to nature** have all been shown to have significant benefits to both your physical body and mental well-being. In no small part, this is because it requires that you are outside, lightly active, in quiet reflection, and unplugged from your devices. These activities are all great on their own, but when put together, they create a potent cocktail for self-healing.

One of my favorite quotes is from Thich Nhat Hanh in his book, *The Miracle of Mindfulness*. Thich Nhat Hanh writes: "People usually consider walking on water or in thin air a miracle. But I think the real miracle is not to walk either on water or in thin air, but to walk on earth. Every day we are engaged in a miracle which we don't even recognize: a blue sky, white clouds, green leaves, the black, curious eyes of a child—our own two eyes. All is a miracle."[18]

So go take a walk, hang at the beach, gaze at the stars, ski down a mountain, or catch the sunrise from your patio with your early morning coffee. Be grateful for the perfect beauty that surrounds you, and let yourself feel a nature-induced joy. I don't need to be a doctor to be qualified to tell you to go outside and enjoy this beautiful planet as it is today, while we still can.

TRY THIS

Part 1: Spend a day, or even just a few hours, noting what your mind is telling you. Categorize this information into two buckets: negative and positive. Which area is filling up faster? Now that you can see the general tone of this mental talk, consider if what you hear is worth acting upon or taking seriously. Don't blindly believe your thoughts as the gospel truth.

Part 2: List the healthy activities that bring you joy. Identify if they are small actions like gardening, going to a concert, spending time with your best friend, or big actions like traveling to another country. How can you fit more of the small actions into your day-to-day? How can you make a plan to add more of the big actions to your long-term road map?

Part 3: A critically important part of mental health is to make sure you keep a close eye on how you feel. Treat your mental health like your physical health. Consider going for regular mental checkups, and make sure you always seek therapy or professional help if needed. Early treatment of mental health conditions and concerns can prevent them from worsening and becoming more difficult to manage.

WHY

Despite not getting the same consideration in society, mental well-being is just as important as physical well-being. Prioritize your mental health by incorporating somatic experiences that make you feel happier, more stimulated, and more peaceful. This ensures that you will have more stability, resiliency, and strength, both in your everyday life and when you are facing down the next big issue that is sure to come flying your way. A healthy mind is foundational to leading a fulfilling and successful life, so make the commitment to prioritize your mental well-being.

Chapter 12:
APPLY YOUR MEDICINE

WE HAVE ALREADY TALKED ABOUT how gnarly life is and how we have almost zero power to control anything but our own reactions to outside factors. So, what do you do when you get swept away by the undercurrent of life—when you lose your balance, when your hand slips off the steering wheel, and you are suddenly off your normal path? Can you spot when this starts to happen? And what do you do to get back in the driver's seat?

Recently, at a week-long family gathering around the Thanksgiving holiday, I found myself in exactly this position. There were a number of compounding factors that had taken hold of me.

1. Many people were staying in my house for an extended amount of time, including a dog that wars with my two cats.

2.   My biggest-to-date speaking gig was coming up the following week, and my thoughts were anywhere but in the zone of merrymaking and revelry.

3.   My general diet was thrown way off by other people's food.

4.   I wasn't able to work out with my usual regularity.

5.   My daughter was home from school for the holiday.

6.   And, and, and . . .

It was a perfect storm for me to slip out of my usual peace of mind and into something . . . not good. It got ugly. I withstood the pressure for as long as I could, but eventually found myself snapping at my mother-in-law, slamming a door on the dog, and having an ugly crying fit in front of my bewildered husband in our bedroom closet. Good look on me, huh? Ugh.

This sort of behavior is so not my style, but it happened. There I was in the closet, and I still had a house full of guests for another few days. I remember letting it out to my husband, who was shocked to learn I was so upset. He wanted to do whatever he could to help. In this case, I knew it was almost 100 percent internal; therefore, there was nothing anyone but me could do to fix this. I was left to ponder, *What do I do when it gets full-on breakdown bad?*

Thankfully, this wasn't my first rodeo. I knew I could patch up my mental state with a two-part harmony. The first part was slowing my roll in that emotional moment, which meant me and my tear-streaked red and puffy face were *not* going to hang out with the rest of the crew that day. Instead, I ran a super-hot bubble bath. I put on some chillhop music and climbed into the tub. I took a couple of hits of my favorite relaxing herb and let myself chill out. I didn't suppress what I was feeling. I let the tears continue to flow. Instead of ignoring or forcibly stopping myself from feeling my emotions, I let them pass through me. Once I had let it all out, I got out of the tub, climbed into my bed, and went to sleep.

The second part of fixing my mental state happened the next day. That morning, I excused myself for a long drive with a beautiful mountain view. I found a cute little coffee shop in a remote town and spent the afternoon in solitude, writing parts of this very book. Removing myself from the triggering situation, I felt recharged inside and out and was able to climb out of the emotional roller-coaster and move on.

Later that afternoon, I returned refreshed and gave myself, and my mother-in-law, a healthy dose of grace and apologies for letting my emotions build up to a breaking point. Sheesh. This is an example of intentional self-healing, and it's the coolest new trick I have.

SPOTTING THE SPIRAL

The spiral is when enough outside factors have hit you, one after another, that you find your emotional responses and behaviors changing in a negative way.

In my case, the days leading up to this episode would have looked like this: I was irritable and frustrated. Innocent questions from my family members were responded to with unfairly clipped and curt statements. My walls had come up, and I retreated inside them. I was less willing to accept any help offered and didn't want to talk. The little things that generally gave me joy were dull. As this negative mental state progressed, I excused myself from social situations, including family dinners and movie nights, and spent more and more time alone.

Do you know what your spiral looks like? Take time and write out what the signs and symptoms are when you start spinning. It is of critical importance that you go through this exercise to recognize it. This way, you can see it when it's there (or better yet, when it's coming) and be able to stop it before it takes full hold of you.

Dr. Leanne Williams of Stanford Medicine[19] writes extensively about identifying your personal signs of stress, which can be used as signals that your mental state is starting to stretch too thin. She has identified types of "short circuits" that occur in our brain when we experience persistent negative stress that we feel we can't control:

* **Rumination** is characterized by extreme brooding and dwelling on negative thoughts and worries.
* **Negative bias** occurs when we end up catastrophizing and getting stuck in a negative fantasy loop about the future.
* **Emotional numbness** is the loss of the ability to feel pleasure from usual activities and goals, which can lead people to find solace in addictive behaviors, including alcohol and drugs.

Do any of these sound familiar? They do to me.

APPLYING THE MEDICINE

After you spot that you are spiraling, the next action is to stop it. This is done by applying your medicine. Depending on the severity of the situation, different timelines and nuances of medicine can be applied, but the high-level recipe for your personal emotional healing process will be the same.

Truth Bomb:

Emotional self-healing is a critically important skill to develop.

Emotional healing is a personal-to-you method of integrating painful emotions and experiences into your life by accepting that they happened, processing what occurred, and then applying a balm of deep reflection, self-compassion, and personal love to the situation. This is often a lengthy process, and attempting a "quick fix" is generally not sustainable. Intentionally uncovering and practicing your unique healing processes will help you authentically move past the issues or stressors that bother you. This is a required course, friends. No skipping this one.

Your medicine isn't anything that can be used as a numbing mechanism. There is a significant distinction between numbing yourself (via consumption of social media, alcohol, drugs, news, or an addictively bad sexual partner, for example) and feeling it, to heal it, by allowing it to flow.

Your medicine is the entire process you follow to bring yourself out of a downward spiral or through a painful situation. This involves accepting what happened and then processing it. This can be accompanied or accelerated by your favorite physical "doing" activities, like taking a walk, working out, going for a drive, resting, or practicing yoga. Mental "being" activities can also help, like working through deep internal reflection, getting lost in your favorite music, amping up your meditative practices, or journaling out your thoughts. Your choices are wide open and highly personal, but the end result is the same: you start feeling better.

TRY THIS

Here are some questions for you to reflect on further. They can give you deeper insights to better understand and support yourself:

* What is your relationship like with yourself? We talk at great length about our relationships with others, but let's start asking about how we are doing with ourselves.
* Do you practice self-care, customized to what you need and with a regular cadence? "Not having time" is not an acceptable excuse.

* Do you honor your body without comparing where you are with where everyone else is? Don't be fooled by filters and Photoshop. Exercise, eat well, treat yourself to a massage. Honor what this body does for you.

* Do you take care of your mind? Do you prioritize your mental health? It is important to allocate time for what makes you happy and lights you up.

* Do you know what your medicine is, and can you spot when you need to apply it?

WHY

Digging deeper into these questions can help you understand your stress triggers and learn how to intentionally self-heal. This will amp up your resilience and propel you toward being able to recover from tricky situations and maintain a more positive relationship with yourself. When that happens, you can finally stop just surviving or getting through and start *thriving*. You can feel more flow and enjoy better relationships with yourself and everyone else.

It is guaranteed that life will continue to throw new, unplanned issues at you. You cannot control any of that. But you can control how you react by beefing up your internal strength. Your goal here is to become an empowered self-care activist. That way, you can lead by example and show others what it looks like when you are your own best friend—emotionally, physically, mentally. This is how you are able to show up in a better way for the people in your world who need you the most.

LIFE LESSON 5:

Expect the Awesome

"There are only two ways to live your life. One is as though nothing is a miracle. The other is as though everything is a miracle."

—Albert Einstein, theoretical physicist, hairstyle influencer, you know this guy by now

LET'S START WITH A TIRED CLICHÉ that I can't resist repeating, so buckle up and humor me. Here it comes. *Today is a new day.* Okay, I know you know that each day is a new day, but seriously, it's a new opportunity to make choices that will lead you all that much closer to living a life you love. The only catch is that you have to go after it. You have to decide that this is the day when you do something that puts you one step closer to living your dreams.

You are who you practice to be, so let's practice expecting the awesome.

This isn't about pretending that the negativity and hatred that seems to be all around us isn't there. You know full well that the world is a spectrum of experiences and events; you are living in it. This is about training your eye and your mind to focus on the good, to note when you do see and hear it so you don't carry the weight of thinking it's all bad out there. The negative events and situations are often far louder than the good ones. Allowing yourself to get overwhelmed by sadness or dismay will affect the energy you bring to your day and everyone you come into contact with. It will also block you from experiencing all the good surrounding you.

We've spoken before about how you cannot be positive all the time, and that's fine; we are all human here. But you can challenge yourself to see the bright side of life. Look at setbacks as necessary learnings. Try to see obstacles as opportunities that help you course correct. When you hear horrible stories, let them be reminders that the world needs you to show up as a happy and healthy person so you can contribute to right-siding the world's energetic balance. The experience of the "not good" helps you value the good even more.

Truth Bomb:

Optimism should be a foundational aspect of your operating system.

Embodied optimism involves two steps. First, commit to maintaining an optimistic outlook and expect good things to come your way. Second, view the world with a trained lens that is fine-tuned to pick up the good things that do happen, both in your world directly and in the world around you. You are looking for the synchronicities, the unexpected delights, the coincidences, and the bold blasts of joy, love, and laughter that come your way. When you look for them, you will find them. By adjusting your approach to daily life so optimism is an undercurrent of all you do, you will create a wholly more positive life for yourself.

If you believe that at the highest level, everything is always working out for your own good, then you can relax the need to control situations around you. You can spend more time flowing and observing rather than resisting and forcing.

I bet by now you have heard about the Law of Attraction, the principle that states "like attracts like." This means that similar energies are drawn to each other. So, if you are walking around with a doom-and-gloom, woe-is-me mindset, that's what you'll get more of. On the other hand, if you are upbeat and excited about life, you will find plenty of evidence that proves you were right—life *is* meant to be full of excitement. When you wake up to another beautiful new day, it *is* worthwhile to be thankful.

Now, let us work to create a personal orbit of positivity and excitement, so you can be a lighthouse of goodness for those around you. Not only can you up-level your attitude and your energy, but you will become a magnet to attract more of the great stuff you are giving out. Let's do it.

As a start, I challenge you to take notes about the good things that happen to you and around you. These can be big or small—anything that feels good. Write them down or send them as texts to yourself, and start an ongoing list of everything you enjoyed throughout your day. It may look something like this:

* I woke up safe and warm in my comfy bed.
* My husband had my coffee ready for me, and it was *just* the way I like it.
* I found a five-dollar bill on the street today.
* I heard an uplifting story on the news.
* I really nailed that presentation.

* That client call went super well . . . hello, upsell!
* My daughter gave me the sweetest hug.
* I get to have dinner and drinks with friends tonight—here come the belly laughs!

Chapter 13:
LIVING LIFE ON PURPOSE

ONCE, IN COLLEGE, a good friend asked me what I wanted to do when I "grew up." I told him I wanted to have a family, to be a mother, a wife, and to have a beautiful home. He looked at me with curiosity and asked: Why then was I going to college? It was a great question. Killing time, perhaps? Wasting my parents' money? Maybe because it was the only post-high school option I was given? It *was* a way for me to live away from home and experience the next big thing, so there I was.

Ironically enough, I became a single mother right out of college. My fledgling career in social work was barely earning enough money to make ends meet for myself, and now there was a baby to support. My son's father was not helping at the time in any way. So this was on me. My answer was to work myself to the bone. I was the first one into work and the last one out.

I jumped from social work to technology to make more money. I took on whatever additional responsibilities were given to me and signed up for stretch projects. I never said no. Over the next few years, my efforts were rewarded, and I received a quick series of raises and promotions.

I ended up building my career out of necessity but found along the way that I was really good at it. Determined to excel, I took on managerial responsibilities and built up teams of some fantastic people. That long-ago conversation with my friend in college when I said I'd likely be a mother and homemaker was ancient history, gathering a decade of dust in the rearview mirror. That is, until I met my now husband and we decided to do two massive things at the same time: start a business and have a baby.

The business was a web and mobile application development shop. The baby was our darling daughter. Both grew simultaneously for years until the pressures of doing both together became too much. Remember the ugly crying fit in the car I described in the first few pages? That occurred around the same time my husband and I decided we needed to make a change. We made the tough choice to wind down the business. He took a new, higher-paying job, and when he did, he told me it would be my choice what I did next. Did I want to stay home full time with our daughter?

So all these years later, with the support of a wonderful, loving man, I was presented with the opportunity to actually live what I had envisioned long ago. I took my husband up on this offer, but almost immediately found that it wasn't right for me. I couldn't *just* stay home with the baby. After these years of establishing myself personally and professionally, I found that I was missing something by not working. I adored being home with my daughter, being more present and available for my husband, and being able to better manage the home, but something was missing. Where were the professional challenges, the work projects, the new missions? I quickly realized that being a stay-at-home mother was not for me and happily stepped back into the workforce.

How we spend our time, personally and professionally, is important. This topic goes beyond having a career. It can expand into your life's mission, your creative undertakings, and your approach to what you do on a daily basis. If you don't know where you are going, the bumps and twists in the road of life will end up etching out a new path, and you'll end up . . . wherever. Since life is in constant motion, it can take you someplace you never expected or intended. Maybe that will work out okay for you, but who wants to leave something as important as your life's direction up to chance? You can prevent that by having a plan.

Do you think it takes too much time or is too big of a risk to have a goal that you are working toward? I would argue that it's more of a risk to sit passively by while your life clock counts down.

Truth Bomb:

The easy road leads nowhere.

People are often worried about change in their lives, but actually, staying in the same place can be a far more detrimental decision when it comes to finding true fulfillment in life. Stalling out on the easy road of life is a great way to ensure that you never grow, never change, and never progress. Abraham Maslow says: "If you plan on being any less than you are capable of being, you will probably be unhappy all the days of your life."[20] Comfort is the killer of dreams. So rather than kill off those potentials, let's take that less-than-easy road and explore what you are really here to do.

Abraham Maslow was a revolutionary psychologist who lived and worked in the early twentieth century. Though other psychologists of the times (looking at you, Freud) studied the mentally ill, Maslow took the opposite approach and instead studied the most successful people he could find—the people who were excelling in life.

In *Toward a Psychology of Being*, Maslow wrote about his discovery that the healthiest people who flourished and enjoyed consistent happiness were those who were "motivated by trends to self-actualization."[21] Self-actualization is defined by *Merriam-Webster* as "an ongoing actualization of potentials, capacities and talents, as fulfillment of a mission, as a fuller knowledge of, and acceptance of, a person's own intrinsic nature and an unceasing trend towards unity."

So, the people who are the happiest are making steady, determined progress toward a personal goal, and even deeper happiness is achieved if the goal involves helping our fellow human beings.

Having a personal goal certainly helps you make big life decisions, as you are able to weigh outcomes against whether or not your goal would be furthered.

If you want your life to be meaningful, then what you do each day in your life matters. A question becomes crystal clear: What is your personal goal? As American Poet and Pulitzer Prize Winner Mary Oliver asks: "What is it that you want to do with your one wild and precious life?"[22]

Let's get specific about what you are here to do.

THE PURPOSE

Q. How do you figure out what your life's purpose should be?

A. Look to your passion. What positive things do you naturally do when no one is paying you?

Your purpose can be something big and public, like becoming the president or helping crack the code on systematic homelessness. It can be something internal or personal, like actively appreciating beauty, journaling, or caring for plants. Keep in mind that you can have more than one purpose in your life. Purposes can shift and change as your life shifts and changes. Stay open to the fact that whatever lights you up today may be quite different from what you'll gravitate toward a few years from now.

If you are unsure here, then return to your stillness. The quiet, still voice within you is always trying to guide you. This is a perfect question for your guidance: What is my purpose in life?

One resource for those who need help figuring this out is to explore *ikigai*—the Japanese philosophy for finding your purpose. Ikigai literally means "reason for being." This methodology can help you identify the sweet crossroads of something you are good at, *plus* something you love doing, *plus* something the world needs, *plus* something you can get paid for. There are books and exercises on this topic that will help you go incredibly deep.

To solidify what you are discovering about yourself, try writing out your personal mission statement. A personal mission statement **defines your purpose in life**. It also explains your identity and values. In essence, it's a statement about who you are and how you want to live. They are generally short—think one to three sentences. And this will likely not change much, as it comes from your depth.

My purpose: To provide inspiration and education around whole life self-care to help people unlock their personal power and live incrementally better, kinder, more harmonious lives.

With your purpose in mind, you can now start to identify your goals.

THE GOALS

Goals are achievable, smaller, more actionable steps that support you toward living the truth of your purpose.

One of my goals is to maintain a speaking career. Another is to write a book.

Identifying your purpose and goals is the aspiration, the dreaming, the visioning of it all—the joy, excitement, and the fun. Man, do I love to plan these! The harder part is coming up next: taking action.

TAKING ACTION

When I began to write *The Well Within*, I was so excited to take on a new, huge challenge. I had only written shorter-form content over the years, but I knew what I wanted to say and was ready to challenge myself to do something big. I began by compiling my notes; I took a writing masterclass and worked with a writing coach to create a great outline. I even set down a rough timeline of deliverables for myself to stay on track. However, as often happens, life immediately got in the way.

Despite my best-laid plans and intentions, I wasn't meeting my goals. My "real" job had kicked up its intensity with many new projects that took most of my computer time to complete.

My personal life was busy with my kids, lots of back-to-back travel, and obligatory events. It was so much at once, and though I knew writing the book was the right next step for me, I couldn't make it happen. So instead of making small, incremental progress, I began to shy away from the project overall.

I justified my lack of action by convincing myself it would be too hard to shift brain gears from family mode into business mode and then back into writing mode. I prioritized everything else I had to do ahead of my personal goal. Even though I still felt the pull of the writing process, each day, I turned my back on it.

It wasn't long before these routine nos began to catch up with me. I felt my emotions taking a downturn in a slight but consistent and troubling way. By ignoring my inner voice and bottling up this creative project, the goal that had once jazzed me up and made me excited began to eat me up and make me unhappy.

A quote that has always stayed with me is from the Gospel of Thomas, where Jesus says: "If you bring forth what is within you, what you bring forth will save you. If you do not bring forth what is within you, what you do not bring forth will destroy you."[23] This is what was happening to me.

The generally accepted life path that our mainstream society operates from doesn't leave much room for creativity or personal growth. So many people keep their gifts, dreams, and aspirations bottled up within themselves, where they do nothing but rot. Over time, the inevitable unhappiness—and social proof of other people not living their best lives either—doesn't seem so unusual. It's just accepted and owned and becomes a part of you. *Do not let this be you.*

Creation is your birthright. It's the highest expression of our humanness. It sets us apart from all of the other creatures roaming the Earth. You do not need to be a traditional artist to be creative. Allowing yourself the pleasure of being fully immersed in what you are doing is creative. Hatching new, exciting ideas from your depth is creative. Seeking out more and striving to do better is creative. If you have a dream in mind, I implore you to do whatever it takes to give that beautiful dream wings. Go on a retreat or take a vacation by yourself. Take a psychedelic and break down whatever barrier is there. At all costs—and with critical urgency—I implore you to break free from what is holding you back.

Truth Bomb:

There is never a perfect time to start moving toward your goal, so you have to start from where you are right now.

If we always waited for the perfect timing before taking action, we would be waiting forever, and nothing would get done because the "perfect timing" doesn't exist. At best, we can survey our life situation and make a good guess about when we might start. But waiting isn't advisable. First of all, dream chasing takes time, and we don't know how much of that we've got. Second of all, time will pass anyway, whether or not we take steps toward our goals. We can look up one day and see that we've made real progress, or we can look up one day and wish we would have started long ago. Your feet are always at the starting line; it's up to you to decide when to step over the threshold.

In my case, those negative feelings inspired me to get back to work. I needed to buckle down and create a new plan, which started with forgiving myself for not following through with the original plan. I re-outlined what needed to get done and started again by taking small steps toward my goal. I adhered to it as best I could. There were ups and downs and life interruptions, for sure.

You are reading *The Well Within* right now, so it's clear I did finish it. It's now a piece of physical evidence to myself that I can do what I don't initially know how to do and what I don't seem to have time to do. If I did it, you can do it too. The keys to reaching your goals are hard work, consistency, and not giving up. The miles it takes to reach a goal can only happen with one small, determined step after another.

The final key is to believe in yourself enough to take the leaps. To go out on a limb and make things happen. You can't wait for the confidence to start working toward the goal. The confidence will be built as you work toward the goal.

TRY THIS

Step 1: Identify Your Purpose

What is it that interests you and excites you? What are you called to do? You'll know what your true purpose is when it lights you up like a Christmas tree from the inside out. Write it down, sit with it, see how it feels. If it still resonates when you come back to it a few more times, that, or something along those lines, could be your purpose.

Step 2: Identify the Goal(s)

What are some goals you can set for yourself that would bring you closer to living your purpose? Draw up a list of a few big goals and put the purpose at the top. Keep this list around where it can easily be seen, so it stays top of mind.

Step 3: Rough Out the Plan

After identifying your purpose and your goal(s), it's time to craft a preliminary plan to hold yourself accountable for how you will start moving forward.

What is one step you can take today to start working toward your goal(s)?

What is the next big milestone in your plan?

Scratch it up; put it together to the best of your ability with what you know now. Reminder: *This does not need to be perfect to work.* It will inspire you to take action, and that action will dictate change (if necessary) along the way. You want this change! It means you are honing in (aka getting closer!) on what you need to do to live your purpose.

Step 4: Take Regular Action

Now for the harder, but far more rewarding, part: Take the first step. And then, take the next step. Get into the habit of actually doing it—not only thinking or dreaming. Repetitive doing creates habits, and habits weave together to make up the fabric of your life. When you are habitually moving toward a goal, you will start to feel the emotional and mental benefit—and the Universe will step in to help push you along. Be brave and courageous enough to follow your action plan steadily. The action you take is the real benefit because it forces you to leave your comfort zone and remove yourself from the dream-killing "easy road." You will learn new skills, meet new people, and terraform your life in a whole new way.

WHY

To become a self-actualized person who is driving toward a goal, you need to stay flexible and be open to the process. Be ready to adjust and rewrite the plan as needed. Be ready for the goal or even the purpose to change. Be ready to feel the rewards when you don't stop taking action. Keep your heart open. When it gets tiring, you rest, but you don't quit. The world desperately needs more people who are willing to follow their dreams and operate from a place of purpose.

Chapter 14:
BELIEVING IN
YOURSELF

WHEN I STARTED HEALTHY WOMEN LEADERS, my first idea to begin gathering a community was to hold an event. It was going to be a small, local event in the Denver area. I found the space, found the amazing woman I would interview, and we set a date. I was excited and impassioned by what I was going to do, but the thought of getting people to actually show up became a huge source of anxiety for me. I was in new territory and felt nowhere near confident. I had been going in circles about each and every scenario in which my event might fail: how bad it would be or how the few stragglers who actually showed up would roll their eyes and regret their attendance. I was lost in my head, and it wasn't a friendly place to be.

A couple of weeks before the event, I woke up in a panic attack in the middle of the night. My heart was racing, my head was spinning, and I felt at a total loss for how I would make this event a success, having no prior experience.

In the midst of my internal chaos, a loud and very stern voice rang in my mind: "Well, you have to believe in yourself." This one-liner of a deep internal truth stopped me in my mental tracks. It made me consider: Do I actually believe in myself? Above all else, do I think I can pull this off? The answer was a feeble and not-very-confident yes, but it was enough to help me pull out of the tailspin and right myself. I got back to sleep that night and worked hard over the next two weeks to promote the event.

We ended up having forty people show up, and the event went exceptionally well. The interview was invigorating and inspiring. The food and drinks were on point. Many people made wonderful new networking connections that evening. I received great feedback from the attendees. It was a success.

I went on to host dozens of events before the COVID-19 pandemic stopped all in-person gatherings. I then transitioned to online events and interviews and haven't stopped since. On that dark night, I desperately needed that internal reminder to believe in myself. Maybe it's you who needs to hear it now? Do you believe in yourself?

There are three key truth bombs to keep in mind as you get ready to do a hard thing:

Truth Bomb:

Impostor Syndrome is a bitch, but not a blocker.

Impostor syndrome is a very real and widespread problem for people who are stretching themselves beyond their comfort zone. It is the unfriendly voice of your inner critic trying to convince you that you are not the badass you hope to be. The good news is that it's not based in reality and can be overcome.

Impostor syndrome is a phenomenon in which an individual doubts their skills, talents, or accomplishments and has a persistent and internalized fear of being exposed as a fraud. *Personal saboteur for one, your table is ready.*

The antidote to impostor syndrome is self-confidence, so if you are struggling here, you need to beef up your belief in yourself. There are lots of ways to enhance your belief in yourself. To name a few:

* Read personal development books (oh, look at you, already crossing this one off the list), listen to podcasts, and watch motivational videos.
* Talk it out with a mentor, advisor, or trusted friend. Being able to address what you are going through verbally is a form of owning it, and it gives the other person the opportunity to assure you that you are, indeed, a boss in your own right with limitless potential and possibility.
* Remind yourself that you did earn your spot at whatever literal or figurative table you are now (or want to be) sitting at. It wasn't luck that got you to where you are. You've got as much right to be there as everyone else.

Social media is a great way to fuel the crisis of confidence you may be feeling, so if impostor syndrome is kicking you in the gut, then maybe it's time to steer your attention away from the socials where everything looks perfect and effortless. It's tough to compare your real life to someone else's highlight reel, so please don't waste your time in that loop.

Check if the impostor syndrome you are feeling is even yours or if it is an internalized stereotype or prejudice. Many people report feeling impostor syndrome because they never saw anyone who looked like them doing that job or taking on that role (i.e., an indigenous woman in a C-level position). Well, you are there now, so if this is the root cause of your insecurity, flip your focus and serve as a visual example for others that this is what it looks like when you (insert your descriptors here) are crushing it at this (insert your role here).

A quote that rings true for me is this: "You can't be distracted by comparison if you are captivated by purpose," as stated by author and speaker Bob Goff.[24] Having a purpose, as explained in the previous chapter, will give you direction and a little boost in the self-confidence tank because you are working on something bigger than yourself.

Finally, when you feel or hear the impostor syndrome kicking in, try to use those negative feelings as a call to self-acceptance and self-love. This is a great example of when you can apply your medicine and make sure taking care of yourself is your number one top priority.

Truth Bomb:

Intuition is an incredibly useful tool at your disposal.

Your intuition is your innate ability to know something internally without the need for physical or verbal proof. It is an inborn guidance system that comes pre-programmed on your Earth Suit. It can guide you, pull you, and inform you. It can help you make decisions, find your way, and discern the quality of characters in your life—but only when you trust it and follow its advice.

Unlike impostor syndrome, which costs precious brain space and is not real, intuition carries a double benefit: it's highly valuable and costs you nothing at all. Intuition is defined by *Merriam-Webster* as the ability to understand something immediately, without the need for additional information or backup. This can show up as a hunch or a gut feeling. It can be felt as a pull to do something or a repulsion away from something. Intuition can be a lot more useful than just thinking about someone right before they contact you. It can be harnessed and used as an effective decision-making methodology in your life.

Your intuition has always been there for you, though most of us forgot about it or neglected it along the rocky pathway of growing up. Rational thought and empirical evidence have always been given a higher priority in our society over emotional intuition. I believe there is an important place for both rational and intuitive thought. When you remember how to tune back into your internal navigation system, you unlock the ability to answer your own pressing questions from within.

To intentionally access your intuition, follow these four steps: pause, ask, listen, act.

PAUSE: The first step to tapping your intuition, especially when you are not used to it, is to pause, get quiet, and be still. This can be done during meditation or by setting yourself up in a quiet place where you won't be interrupted. This can also happen on a solo walk, hike, or rest in nature.

ASK: After a few moments in your quiet place, ask the question that you are grappling with, such as: Should I move to California? You then consider the possibilities of yes or no. You mentally run through each option in depth and see how you feel as you consider what life would be like if you did or did not move.

LISTEN: The choice that isn't right will evoke negative feelings of anxiety, worry, angst, or concern. The choice that is right will evoke positive feelings such as excitement, hope, possibility, and wonder. Although a choice is right, a feeling of nervousness may accompany the "Yes, do it!" category. Nervousness is natural with any change because it lives on the other side of the excitement coin. So don't confuse this feeling as being negative, and don't allow it to be a deterrent.

Intuition can also speak to you through signs. Signs are clues, images, or coincidences that appear around you in your day-to-day life and are related to the question or topic for which you are seeking guidance. When you feel or see something that seems important, know that it is important, as it is what your mind picked up on. Write it down. Piece the thoughts, feelings, and signs together to uncover the inner direction.

ACT: The last step is also the most important—act on the direction you've been given. This is the keystone that will help you build up trust in your intuition. As you follow this powerful guidance, you will gather case law that shows how your decisions always work out in one way or another when they're directed from within.

Your intuition is the valuable inner voice that speaks in whispers. Take care to tune into this quiet superpower and see where it leads you.

Truth Bomb:

The only thing you should ever fake is confidence.

As a general rule, I would not recommend that you fake it *except* in terms of confidence. Unless you are a superhero whose magic knows no boundaries (as I'm sure some are), there will be times when you have to fake being confident before you can feel the actual confidence. This is great because it means you are stretching yourself toward something new.

We all know that growth happens outside of our comfort zone. If you find yourself nervous and uncomfortable because you are doing something new, that's great. If you have to be brave and fake a smile to go do a hard thing, that's great too. You are right where you need to be. This is the fast track to positive growth.

I know firsthand how rough it is to push ourselves to do the hard new things. My first few speaking gigs were a *major* source of brain drain and anxiety for me. Yet, the rewards from stretching myself have been incredible.

Although that piece of the process isn't for the faint of heart, the relief and accomplishment you feel on the other side is worth every bit of angst you experience trekking there. Like a muscle that is worked, develops a tear, and grows back a bit bigger, you have earned a level up to your current skill set by stretching yourself past your previous point.

TRY THIS

Whatever it is that you have on your goals list, whatever your biggest dream is, why *can't* you do it? What is the difference between you and all the others who have done this before? Are there any specific barriers you have to overcome to make this happen? Let's honestly answer that question in this exercise now.

* Grab a notebook and write your goal at the top of the page.
* Below that, draw three columns on the page.
* In the first column, make a list of everything you feel is holding you back from achieving that goal.

✳ In the second column, write out whether these barriers are real or perceived.

✳ In the third column, if they are real, identify what would need to happen to help you get past that barrier.

Regarding the barriers that you marked as perceived, isn't it time to *stop perceiving in this way*? Own the fact that you have an internal narrative about why you think this could be a blocker, but move forward anyway. The magic is in the action, so lace up and start moving.

WHY

To sum it up, one of the key ingredients for any goal-chasing, self-actualizing human is a hefty helping of trust. Not only in the Universe or that "things will all work out okay," but specifically in yourself because you are the one who has gotten you through all of the other tough stuff up to this point. This is how true self-confidence is born.

When facing a challenging situation, you can be scared or nervous while remaining firm in the knowledge that you can do whatever you set your mind to do. Impostor syndrome can flare up, and that's okay. Mistakes are a part of the process and can be extremely valuable if we learn from them. Nothing needs to be perfect because perfection doesn't exist. Flex into your intuition to guide you as needed. Power through uncertainty with confidence (faked until it's real) that there is nothing you can't do. You have been unsure plenty of times before and still gotten to where you are now. You are the key to your success.

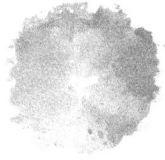

Chapter 15:
BELIEVING IN THE BENEVOLENT

MY YOUNG DAUGHTER WANTS so badly to believe in magic. She thinks about it often and asks me: "Mama, is magic *real*?" I know in my heart that it is, but man, do I struggle to find the words that will make sense to someone so eager to fly, to have a pet unicorn, and to turn into a mermaid.

"Magic is real for the people who believe in it," I tell her. She assures me that she does believe, but she is losing faith because she didn't see the things she wanted magic to provide.

"Magic doesn't work the way you think it will, but that doesn't mean it's not real," I explain. I give her examples that mean something to me. Here she is, my great dream, manifested. Here we are, in our beautiful, warm, and safe home, full of love. The unbounded potential surrounding us—surrounding her in her "just getting started" life—is absolute magic to me. The beauty of a sunrise, a rainbow, the laughter between great friends, *my God*, there are limitless examples of magic around us! The proof of magic is the fact that everything I once wished for has become, with an eye on the goal and a hefty amount of effort taken in the right direction, tangibly real.

I shared this with my eager young daughter, but after checking her legs again and seeing that they still hadn't turned into a mermaid tail, she wandered away, highly mistrustful of her Mom's bizarre advice. I firmly stand behind it, though. Magic *is* real, but just like I told her, you have to believe in it to fully see or feel it for yourself.

One of the great gifts of getting older is perspective. You are able to look back on the events of your life and better understand why they happened and where they led you.

When I look back to my days of being a broke single mother, fumbling around and trying not to upset my precariously balanced life, I can now see the gifts I received during that time in the form of hard-earned, based-on-personal-experience truths.

* I developed a steadfast work ethic that propelled my career forward in ways I'm still astonished by.
* I earned an unshakable belief that I could do whatever I set my mind to, which helps me to this day as I take on huge, hairy goals.

✳ I hatched a deep resolve that I wouldn't give up no matter what, as I'd seen firsthand that sticky situations will, in time and through effort, become life lessons learned.

I wouldn't give back these understandings for anything, though at the time, I was living in a brain fog and was more or less miserable. These learnings have helped me fully embody that we humans can always have a hand in directing the trajectory of our lives. Hello, empowerment. Aren't you looking powerful today?

Who we are, as we sit here today, is made up of our personal collection of past experiences coupled with our reaction to what has occurred and, perhaps most importantly, what we learned from them. An important part of believing in the benevolent is to trust that life is always working out in our favor.

Flipping your thinking from "Life is happening *to* me" to "Life is happening *for* me" is a huge unlock that will open you up to a deep new level of trust. This helps you take your foot off the must-control-the-outcome pedal and instead flex into curiosity about what lesson is baked into each situation for you. When you allow the unfolding of life, you are far better able to enjoy the ride.

Truth Bomb:

Life is happening for you, not *to* you.

We all know that life is tough—full of ups and downs, plot twists, and sudden turns. Without keeping sight of the overall, higher-level pathway you are on, you can feel lost or out of control. Look deeper to see that the past events in your world have each led you to where you are now. Take the lessons you've learned, forgive yourself and others for past grievances, and keep your eyes on the horizon. Great things are coming!

RELEASING CONTROL

Establishing trust in the Universe allows you to release your need to control the people and events around you. This is great, because that shit is pointless and exhausting. When you trust that everything is working out as it should be, you feel okay when things don't go the way you envisioned, because you know that something better is on its way. The desires that you have are enough to direct your life along its proper path, even if the outcomes don't match your plan. This is co-creating your human experience with the Universe, Source, Spirit, God, the Benevolent, your higher power within. Whatever you can comfortably call it, there is a positive force aligning everything on your behalf for your own highest good—if you choose to see it that way.

Having belief in the goodness and support of the Universe helps you regain your personal power by relinquishing your need for minute control. Look at everything that happens without your involvement. Your bodily functions happen without your control. The seasons in nature change without your control. Celestial events happen without your control. They are all guided by divine support, and they all flow just the way they're intended. You can relax into that same divine support and enjoy a deeper connection with the flow of life.

GETTING INTENTIONAL (AKA MANIFESTING FOR BEGINNERS)

Here is an interesting paradox: you can simultaneously take the reins as a creator of your life while releasing your white-knuckle grip on the specific outcomes.

When you have established a level of trust in the Universe to support you, then you can get really direct with specific intentions.

This is not actionless dreaming or hoping, which highlights the lack of what you want. This is getting really clear about what you want and then *declaring what you intend to happen,* with the caveat that you are always open to whatever else may be best for you. This sets the Universe in motion to begin arranging things, so your declared desire, or whatever is better, has a pathway to get to you. It's like putting in your food order at a restaurant. You state what you want, and then you move on without a worry because you know that a plateful of food will appear in front of you soon.

The request that you make could be something as specific as "a cherry red '78 Mustang convertible," but in my experience, a far better way to make requests when talking directly to the Divine is to ask for a feeling or a state instead of something on-the-nose specific. Something like: "I want to let go of these negative feelings and make space for better thoughts" or "I'm ready to access a deeper level of happiness" or "I don't want to be afraid of this anymore."

From there, you have to do your part of the work by preparing for the eventual arrival of what you've asked for. This involves a heavy amount of mental visioning, emotional feeling, and adopting new habits into your daily routine that prepare your mind, body, and environment for what you've declared.

Then—and this is a tricky part, but by now, you are getting good at letting go—you let that specific intention go and continue on as usual. You continue with whatever new habits you've adopted and a healthy dose of trust that what you are seeking is now also seeking you. You know it's only a matter of time until it shows up. This is manifesting for beginners, and it works because you mentally envision, prepare for, and expect to get what you want while staying open to the fact that something better may be coming along.

RECOGNIZING SUPPORT

There are very specific times in my life when I start to see signs and synchronicities with a frequency that suggests I'm being supported by something other than my fumbling human self. These signs can be an aptly placed quote that I found scrawled on a bathroom wall, a shooting star, a magnificent rainbow, a call from an old friend with news that I needed right then.

This often happens as I'm going through a challenging time. It's as if the Universe is saying, "It's time to learn something important, but I'm right here with you for it." It definitely doesn't mean this learning will come easily or be comfortable. In fact, it usually means the opposite. However, if I can keep in mind that something good is on its way, it helps me work through the tough times that precede the learning.

The support we can feel flows from human to human as well. All life on this planet began from the same conditions, through the same organisms. This means that we are, at our very core elements, deeply connected to each other, to this planet, and to the Universe. Humans get the special privilege to operate as conscious beings, and our consciousness further allows for our connectedness. So don't forget to look for the signs and synchronicities of support among your fellow humans as well.

TRY THIS

To help you amp up your belief in the benevolent, you can look both back into your personal history and ahead into your personal future.

Learning from Past Lessons: Looking back at your life, what were one or two major life events that felt detrimental while they were happening, but now, in hindsight, you are able to see the lesson they were there to teach you? Take some time to journal about these events. Clearly state what you learned from them. If this doesn't come easy, take your time to consider significant moments in your life. There is always a gift wrapped up inside a hard lesson, if you peel it back far enough.

Expecting the Future Good: A key practice to beef up your belief in the benevolent is to expect good things to happen every day and then note when they do. Keep a running log (literally, write it out) of everything helpful, positive, synchronistic, and fun that occurs in your life. Make note of what it feels like when this happens—this is the feeling of being supported.

WHY

No matter when you are reading this, you are standing on the door-step that can lead to something new, great, and exciting. Allow yourself to be optimistic and embody the belief that you can trust that good things are coming your way. Go deeper and *expect* good things. Look for them and then note and celebrate them when they arrive.

You are here to fully experience this life. You can take an active role in shaping your life to be whatever you want. When you start to acknowledge the lessons baked into each situation you experience, you come to understand that there are no mistakes. Things really do happen for a reason. Flexing into this level of trust and faith is a tough muscle to develop, but when you do, that mindset is yours to keep, and it will cushion you for the rest of your life. Trusting life then becomes a supportive push to help you keep stepping outside of your comfort zone.

The world outside is a reflection of what you are thinking and feeling on the inside. Get solid in your belief that something awesome is always right around the corner. When that is true in your heart, it will also become true in your world.

CONCLUSION: A NEW WAY OF LIVING

"The best day of your life is the one on which you decide your life is your own. No apologies or excuses. No one to lean on, rely on, or blame. The gift is yours—it is an amazing journey—and you alone are responsible for the quality of it. This is the day your life really begins." [25]

—Bob Moawad, businessman and author who deeply obsesses about human effectiveness

Kudos to you for sticking with this book to the end! There's something significant to be acknowledged about finishing something in today's always-on, can't-stop-won't-stop world.

Now that we have gone through the full list of the Five Key Life Lessons, a whole bunch of truth bombs, and a barrage of loving but firmly doled out, somewhat-solicited advice, I hope you have found at least a few practices you can incorporate into your daily life. I believe it takes only small modifications to start feeling better each day.

We all have space to make a few minor adjustments to the way we live, but we humans oftentimes have a difficult time committing to change. At this point, you may be feeling some resistance, asking yourself: Why should I bother? Why should I take the time and make the effort to practice radical self-care? Here are my top three reasons:

1. **We do it for ourselves**, to overcome our intrinsic bullshit and live better lives. We have heaps of unlearning to do, but because we are aware of it, the work is already halfway done. We know that curveballs are coming, so we work to fortify ourselves from the inside out to withstand whatever might be flung our way. We realize that the only control we have is over our own reactions and emotions, so that is where we put our effort.

We commit to live our best possible lives by drawing directly from our place of personal power.

❋ **We do it for those around us,** so we can be better to them and for them every day. Think of it like this: I'm helping ME so I can better serve WE. Mother Teresa said: "If you want to change the world, go home and love your family." That's exactly it! Our families and friends are those closest to us, so they feel what we give off the most. We can be productive and enthusiastic. We can be clear and authentic. We can become viral bombs of goodness in our inner circles. Ripples of our happiness will pulse through them and on to everyone they meet. Kindness has the power to become as contagious as a virus.

We commit to using our personal power to show up as best we can for those around us.

❋ **We do it for the collective,** so we can contribute goodness to our society. As people who are waking up in life, we have a responsibility to model what it looks like to be a happy, healthy, and thriving human, despite the crazy that is happening around us. The large-scale global change that our species desperately needs has to start with one person making one small change at a time. This is how we spackle up the cracks in a broken world.

We commit to contributing our personal power to help light up the world.

If this non-psychologist, non-nutritionist, non-meditation teacher, non-spiritual guide, who is a swamped, hardworking mother, wife, and businesswoman, can sketch together a better way to live, you certainly can too. I took a stand against burnout and refused to get swept away in the creeping tsunami of daily life. It has made every bit of difference for me.

I know this stuff can be tough. You have to shake hands with your inner demons, crawl through your dark shadows, and own up to your part in perpetuating them. This takes time, dedication, courage, and bravery. But embarking on this mission is the greatest adventure of your life because it pulls you to do, see, and experience *more*. To go deeper into the well within. It's not that what you have now is not good enough; it's that there is always more depth available to you.

The truth is that we get only so long on this beautiful planet. Our fleeting lives will fade away at some point, but not yet. Not today. The key is to live it right now while we can. To remember the transient nature of it all and wildly chase after our dreams.

So go forth and gobble up new experiences! Meet new people, try new things, stay open and curious, and maintain a sense of trust throughout it all. Have deeper relationships, starting with yourself. Find what you love and what you don't so you can intentionally craft your life into the version that fits just right for you.

I know this isn't for everyone. Change can be terrifying. Many people are not okay with change or the inevitable uncertainty that comes with it. They would rather maintain the status quo they are currently living, whether it's right for them or not. To each their own, but personally, I know change sparks growth, so I choose to embrace it. I hear my inner calling, and I want to see where it leads me. I want to cannonball down the rabbit hole and see what Wonderland is actually like. And since you found *The Well Within* right when you needed it, my hunch is that this applies to you too.

I believe in you because I believe in myself, and we are all made of the same stuff. The only difference is what we choose to do about it.

I intend to live with a deep connection to myself, to those around me, to Nature, to Spirit. I embrace change and commit to exploring it and exploiting it. I want to craft my life intentionally. To have a great variety of experiences and live a life beyond my wildest imagination. This is what I stand for—what do *you* stand for?

What will you get up and be passionate about? How can you help the world? And what is stopping you from doing that now? If you are content where you are, then enjoy that and don't forget it. But if you want to go and do more, honor that gift of adventure and heed the call. There are an infinite number of ways you can inspire personal development and growth, and you don't need to uproot your life to do it. Growth—isn't *that* what we are here to do? We were planted on this Earth to challenge ourselves, to learn, to step beyond the boundaries of our comfort zones.

This is your reminder to listen deeply and with great consideration to what is calling you. Rumi said: "That which you seek is also seeking you." Something is seeking you, whether it's a new relationship, getting a promotion at work, figuring out how to incorporate your new business, or having to learn a language quickly so you can order an adventurous new meal. Whatever it is, it's there because it'll take you a step forward on the journey of life. Don't ignore it.

By making the commitment to taking stellar care of yourself inside and out, you can live your life from a place of true happiness, health, and abundance. You will be able to intentionally self-heal to work through the tough stuff without rolling over or giving up. This is how you unlock your personal power and make magic happen. This is how you dive deeply into the well within. You will shine from the inside out and operate from a deep, self-fulfilling place of contentment and unlimited possibility.

Though this book has come to an end, I hope it feels like more of a beginning. A call to action to start *right now* to craft your life into exactly what you want it to be, starting from the inside out. Make a masterpiece out of the greatest blank canvas you will ever own.

This much I know is true: My learning-loving-living adventure is just getting started. My wish for you from here is to thrive as a hardworking human and leader in all aspects of your life. May we all go forth and light up this crazy world with our excitement, goodness, and joy.

NOTES

1   Louisa May Alcott, *Little Women*, (Massachusetts: Roberts Brothers, 1868).

2   Erik Stensland, *The Journey Beyond* (Colorado: Rocky Trail Press, 2021).

3   *Science of Meditation* documentary: https://www.aspenideas.org/sessions/the-science-of-meditation

4   His Holiness the Dalai Lama, *A Handbook for Living: The Art of Happiness* (New York: Riverhead Books, 2009).

5   McKayla Robbin, *We Carry the Sky* (Self-Published, 2016).

6   Alex Kerai, "2023 Cell Phone Usage Statistics: Mornings Are for Notifications," REVIEWS.org, July 21, 2023, accessed on August 19, 2023. https://www.reviews.org/mobile/cell-phone-addiction/

7   Andrea Hsu, "Women are earning more money. But they're still picking up a heavier load at home," NPR. org, April 13, 2023, accessed on August 26, 2023. https://www.npr.org/2023/04/13/1168961388/ pew-earnings-gender-wage-gap-housework-chores-child-care

8   Marie Kondo, accessed on August 26, 2023, https://konmari. com/

9   Justina Blakely, accessed on August 26, 2023, https://www. justinablakeney.com/

10 Pema Chödrön, *Start Where You Are: A Guide to Compassionate Living* (Colorado: Shambhala Publications, 1994).

11 Pema Chödrön, *When Things Fall Apart: Heart Advice for Difficult Times* (Colorado: Shambhala Publications, 1994).

12 Jennifer Garman, "How Gratitude Can Help You to Overcome Life's Challenges," *Thrive Global*, April 23, 2020, accessed August 19, 2023. https://community.thriveglobal.com/ gratitude-life-challenges-happiness-research-neuroplasticity/

13 Silvia Bellezza, "Conspicuous Consumption of Time: When Busyness and Lack of Leisure Time Become a Status Symbol," 2016. Published by Oxford University Press on behalf of Journal of Consumer Research, Inc. accessed on August 26, 2023. https://business.columbia.edu/sites/default/files-efs/ pubfiles/19293/Conspicuous%20Consumption%20of%20 Time%20JCR.pdf

14 Ram Dass, *Be Here Now* (New Mexico: Lama Foundation, 1971).

15 Elizabeth Dunn, "Helping others makes us happier -- but it matters how we do it," TED Talk, April 2019, accessed August 19, 2023. https://www.ted.com/talks/elizabeth_dunn_helping_others_makes_us_happier_but_it_matters_how_we_do_it

16 Audre Lorde, *A Burst of Light: and Other Essays* (New York: Firebrand Books, 1988).

17 Michael Singler, *The Untethered Soul: The Journey Beyond Yourself* (Oakland: New Harbinger Publications, 2007).

18 Thich Nhat Hanh, *The Miracle of Mindfulness: An Introduction to the Practice of Meditation* (Massachusetts: Beacon Press, 1999).

19 Dr. Leanne Williams, "This New Brain Science Could Help You Unlock Better Mental Health", March 8, 2022, accessed August 23, 2026. https://community.thriveglobal.com/mental-health-biotypes-brain-science-leanne-williams-research-signs-stress/

20 Abraham H. Maslow, *The Farther Reaches of Human Nature* (New York: Penguin/Arkana, 1993).

21 Abraham H. Maslow, *Toward a Psychology of Being* (New York: Wiley, 1998).

22 Mary Oliver, "The Summer Day," *New and Selected Poems, Volume 1* (Massachusetts: Beacon Press, 1992).

23   https://www.goodreads.com/quotes/126072

24   Bob Goff, accessed August 26, 2023, https://www.bobgoff.
     com/

25   Bob Moawad, *The Secret of the Slight Edge: How to Get Out of
     Your Own Way* (London: Aylesbury Publishing, 2007).

ACKNOWLEDGMENTS

THERE ARE MANY PEOPLE in my community who support me, in the writing of *The Well Within* and in life itself. I would never be where I am today without the love, care, and influence of these people. My tribe! I am forever grateful for each of you in so many beautiful ways.

Nolan: My partner in life and love, the man who showed me what true connection genuinely feels, looks, and acts like. You are my rock and constant through the good and bad. I'm so glad we found one another. I love you for all of our time.

Adayden and Zenaya: My children, my staggering loves, my teachers whom I learn so much from every single day.

Mom and Dad: Thank you for modeling what real, lifelong love of learning, reading, and critical thinking involves. I'm so glad that I had you both as my first guides to navigate this wild world.

Jess: My lifelong best friend, a sister by choice, the loyal confi-dante I rely on for advice, encouragement, "I know nothing" expertise, and commiseration. I am humbled that we get to share this whole life experience together. Let's GGG!

Julie: My business partner, mentor, and friend. A wonderfully wild woman who has shown me that being your perfectly imperfect self is what's most important, quickly followed by good friends, great food, belly laughs, endless travel, and ridiculous fun.

Amy: A great mentor who showed me how an unbelievably successful businesswoman can become even greater when she chooses her own health and happiness over business.

Huge thanks to my editor, Donna Mazzitelli, who held me up through this very new process and kept me going with a beautiful blend of encouragement and corrections to make this book into what it has become. It wouldn't have been this complete without you.

Also, thank you to Alison Daley, Elaine Marino, Dori Starnes, Guthrie Gordon, Sol Gordon, Shannon Gordon, Caitlin DeMille, Jory Garrido, Odete Garrido, Freddy Garrido, Julie Hudson, Melissa Kennedy, Kaytia King, and Alexis Goodwin: you have all taught me so much in your own way. I'm so happy to have you in my life.

And to all the closed doors, nos, roadblocks, and upsets that I thought were deterring me from where I should have gone: thank you *so much* for the course correction that steered me to where I really needed to go.

ABOUT THE AUTHOR

KALIA GARRIDO is the founder of Healthy Women Leaders, a national collective that provides inspiration and education for women in leadership to practice radical, whole-life self-care as a critical measure to thriving in a chaotic world.

She is a longtime fitness fan and regular meditator who strives to bring mindfulness into her everyday life. As a married mother of two and owner of multiple businesses, this is how she keeps it all together.

In her business life, Kalia is a driven marketing executive in the ever-changing and fast-paced world of digital transformation and technology.

Learn more at www.HealthyWomenLeaders.com

INVITE KALIA TO
YOUR BOOK CLUB!

AS A SPECIAL GIFT to readers of *The Well Within: Unlocking Your Personal Power Through Radical Self-Care,* Kalia is available to visit your book club either via video conferencing or in person. Please contact Kalia directly at kalia@healthywomenleaders.com to schedule her appearance.

STAY CONNECTED!

To stay connected, you can find Kalia online at:

* **YouTube:** www.youtube.com/@HealthyWomenLeaders
* **Instagram:** www.instagram.com/healthywomenleaders/
* **LinkedIn:** www.linkedin.com/in/kaliagarrido/
* **Website:** HealthyWomenLeaders.com

One last favor ...

If you have been touched by *The Well Within,* please be sure to visit Kalia's Goodreads, Barnes & Noble, and Amazon book pages and leave a review.

Thank you!

ABOUT THE PRESS

MERRY DISSONANCE PRESS is a hybrid indie publisher/ book producer of works of transformation, inspiration, exploration, and illumination. MDP takes a holistic approach to bring books into the world that make a little noise and create dissonance within the whole so ALL can be resolved to produce beautiful harmonies.

Merry Dissonance Press works with its authors every step of the way to craft the finest books and help promote them. Dedicated to publishing award-winning books, we strive to support talented writers and assist them to discover, claim, and refine their distinct voices. Merry Dissonance Press is the place where collaboration and facilitation of our shared human experiences join together to make a difference in our world.

For more information, visit merrydissonancepress.com.